INTO BOOKS

101 Literature Activities for the Classroom

Ron Thomas
Andrew Perry

Gay Wallis

April 1987

Melbourne
Oxford University Press
Auckland

OXFORD UNIVERSITY PRESS

Oxford New York Toronto
Delhi Bombay Calcutta Madras Karachi
Petaling Jaya Singapore Hong Kong Tokyo
Nairobi Dar es Salaam Cape Town
Melbourne Auckland
and associates in
Beirut Berlin Ibadan Nicosia

OXFORD is a trademark of Oxford University Press

First published 1984
Reprinted 1985 three times

National Library of Australia
Cataloguing-in-Publication data:
Thomas, Ron, 1947—
Into books.

ISBN 0 19 554545 1.

1. Literature — Study and teaching (Elementary). I. Perry,
Andrew. II. Title.

372.6'4044

Designed by John van Loon
Cover and illustrations by Terry Denton
Typeset by Syarikat Seng Teik Sdn. Bhd., Malaysia.
Printed in Hong Kong
Published by Oxford University Press, 7 Bowen Crescent, Melbourne

Contents

Introduction

This book is for teachers. It is designed to help them develop an enriched literary environment within the classroom.

The authors are not advocating a rigid approach to the study of literature, but rather an approach which emphasizes informal activity and discussion around those books which teachers read to their children.

Underlying the approach taken in the book, is a framework which suggests particular literary abilities to be aimed for at each of three levels:

Level One: Ages 5–7
Level Two: Ages 8–9
Level Three: Ages 10–12

Literature themes provide one means of linking this framework to the informal approach referred to above. In this book, those literary abilities on which teachers may wish to concentrate, are introduced and developed via themes. The themes have been placed at particular levels, because the authors have found these themes to be successful with children at those levels. However, the treatment of a theme at one level does not preclude its use at other levels, provided that activities and discussion points are developed from literature which is appropriate for children at that level.

The book also includes studies of novels, picture story books, poetry and the work of particular authors.

Explanation of the framework pages

Abilities to be reached

These abilities deal with the elements of literature (characterization, plot, setting, mood, theme and style) which the authors believe teachers should introduce to children. While particular abilities have been listed for particular levels, teachers may wish to select abilities from across levels to meet the needs and interests of their children.

Teaching points

These are suggested focus questions and activities which may be used as a starting point for dealing with particular abilities.

Literary forms appropriate for level

These are the literary forms which the authors feel should be introduced to children at that particular level.

Activities

Detailed literature themes and activities follow each framework page. In developing these themes, select from and adapt the suggested activities to meet the needs and interests of your children.

Level 1 Ages 5–7

Framework for Ages 5–7 literature program

Activities

Themes
    Colour
    Mice
    Bears

Picture story books
    Books by one author
    Single picture-book activities
    Picture-books about one character

Nursery rhymes

Fairy tales

Framework for Ages 5 and 6 literature program

Abilities to be reached	Teaching points	Literary forms appropriate for level
Identify picture story books as a literary form.	Children are to realize that picture-books tell stories with words and pictures.	Picture story Poetry
Verbalize sequence of main events in stories read.	Children retell events using pictures as cues.	Story-telling Nursery rhymes
Identify the main characters from picture story books read.	Who/what was the most important character? Why was he/she more important than others? Draw/paint a series of pictures of main characters. Hang these in cardboard frames as a 'gallery'.	Fairy stories
Describe where the story takes place in particular picture story books.	Draw/paint a scene of this location. Introduce vocabulary related to setting, e.g. country/city.	
Identify strong emotions that occur in picture story books that are read.	How does the person feel — happy/sad? Can you tell from the illustrations which emotion is portrayed? Dramatize facial expressions.	

Framework for Age 7 literature program

Abilities to be reached	Teaching points	Literary forms appropriate for level
Distinguish between picture story and factual books.	Children are to realize that picture-books tell stories with both words and pictures, while non-fiction books are designed specifically to give information. Compare picture story books and factual books on a particular topic.	Picture story Poetry Story-telling Nursery rhymes Fairy stories
Verbalize obvious themes in picture story books.	What is the main idea behind the story? Possible themes at this level include: overcoming fears; friendship; humour.	
Verbalize sequence of main events in stories read.	Dramatize different events in stories read, in sequence. Draw a picture for the beginning, middle and end of the story.	
Identify the main character from particular picture story books and describe chief physical features.	Draw or paint the main character. Compile lists of words to describe characters.	
Describe the locale and setting for a particular picture story book.	Distinguish between past/present/future; here/there. Develop art activities to depict locale.	
Identify strong emotions that occur in a picture story book and explain the contribution of the illustrations to that end.	Do illustrations, through use of colour and line, help create the mood or express the emotion? Draw a sad/happy/angry face.	

THEME
Colour

Session 1

Activities

Compile a list of colour names known by children.

Play 'Colour — I spy'. 'I spy with my little eye, something that is green.'

Using prepared flash cards, play a word and colour-association game.
One child holds up the flash card

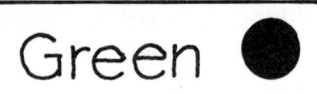

Another child responds with the name of something that is that colour.
Green — grass, frogs, leaves, jelly.
Teams may be formed and the team given one minute to list all items of a given colour. A point is awarded to the team for each item listed.

Read *Mr Rabbit and the lovely present* by Zolotow.

Discuss

Which present would you have preferred?
What else could the little girl have given her mother?
Why didn't the mother like birds in cages?

Session 2

Activities

Sing songs and say nursery rhymes which refer to colour.
For example:
Sing a song of sixpence . . . **black** birds
Baa baa **black** sheep . . .
Little Boy **Blue** . . .
Mary, Mary quite contrary . . . **silver** bells

Teacher tells 'Little Red Riding Hood'. Have the children retell the story as an 'around the grade' story, i.e. one child begins the story and continues until the teacher indicates with a snap of the fingers that the next child should continue the retelling.

Make simple finger puppets to use as future aids to the telling of 'Little Red Riding Hood'.

7

Session 3

Read *The great blueness and other predicaments* by Lobel.

Discuss

When do you think this story happened? How can you tell? Use the illustrations to support your answers.
Where did the story take place?
What methods of transport can you see?
What musical instruments are used by the people?
How did colour affect the mood of the people?

Activities

Classify the colours. They can be listed on charts for display.

Happy Colours	Sad Colours	Angry/Hot Colours
yellow	blue	red
pink	black	orange

Draw the wizard travelling on one of the methods of transport. Use only one colour as Arnold Lobel has done, or draw in pencil or chalk or ink on a coloured sheet of paper.

Session 4

Activities

Students retell *The great blueness and other predicaments* by Lobel.

Act out all of the actions mentioned in the story: mixing, stirring, rowing, riding horses, pedalling bicycles, painting. Prepare cards with statements made by the wizard, or comments likely to have been made by the people.

> With all this yellow, what a perfectly glorious day we are having.

> This yellow is too bright.

Ask children to say them in various moods: sad, angry, feeling unwell, tired, happy.

Session 5

Read *A colour of his own* by Lionni.

Discuss

What methods do animals use to protect themselves? Encourage children to suggest other situations in which the chameleon might change colour.

Read *The mixed-up chameleon* by Carle.

Activity

Draw a mixed-up animal, for example, a yellow horse or a pink cat. Compile these illustrations with labels into a book of 'Mixed-up animals'.

Session 6

Read *Jim and the beanstalk* by Briggs.

Activities

Have each child make a pair of 'rose coloured glasses'. A cardboard frame is cut out, coloured cellophane becomes the lens, string holds the 'glasses' in place.

Make a colour-classification book. Each page of the book includes the childrens' illustrations, or pictures collected from magazines of things that are the selected colour.

Things that are red	🍎 apples stop light 🚦	fire 🚒 engines

Session 7

Read 'The Land of the Bumbley Boo' by Spike Milligan in *Oh such foolishness*.

Discuss

What colours are in the poem?
Is there such a place as the 'Land of Bumbley Boo'?
Do you know of other 'pretend' places?

Activity

Draw a 'Bumbley Boo' zoo.

Read 'What is Pink' by Christina Rossetti in *Poems children will sit still for*.

Discuss

Are the things in this poem 'pretend' like Spike Milligan's poem?

Activity

In the poem Christina Rossetti says, 'What is yellow? Pears are yellow.'
Make a list of other things that we eat that are yellow.

Try to write extra lines for 'What is Pink' using the format
What is _____? A _____
is _____.

Bibliography

Briggs, Raymond *Jim and the beanstalk* (Puffin)

Brooks, Ron *Annie's rainbow* (Collins)

Carle, Eric *The mixed-up chameleon* (Hamilton)

Cole, William (compiler) *Oh such foolishness* (Methuen)

Duvoisin, Roger *See what I am* (World's Work)

Freeman, D. *A rainbow of my own* (World's Work)

Lionni, Leo *A colour of his own* (Armada Picture Lions)

Lobel, Arnold *The great blueness and other predicaments* (Armada Picture Lions)

Ross, T. *Hugo and the man who stole colours* (Andersen)

Schenck de Regniers, B. (compiler) *Poems children will sit still for* (Citation)

Walsh, Amanda *Egrin and the painted wizard* (Penguin)

Zolotow, Charlotte *Mr Rabbit and the lovely present* (Bodley Head/Puffin)

Write the missing colour in the spaces.

Baa Baa _____
sheep have you any wool?

Little _____ Riding Hood
met the wolf on her way
to visit her grandmother.

Snow _____
lived with the seven dwarfs.

How many colours can you find
hidden in this puzzle?
See if you can find eight.

P	I	N	K	A	B	B
U	C	D	E	F	R	G
R	E	D	H	I	O	J
P	K	O	L	Y	W	M
L	G	R	E	E	N	N
E	O	A	P	L	Q	R
S	T	N	B	L	U	E
U	V	G	W	O	X	Y
Z	A	E	B	W	C	D

Little Boy _____
fell asleep under the haystack.

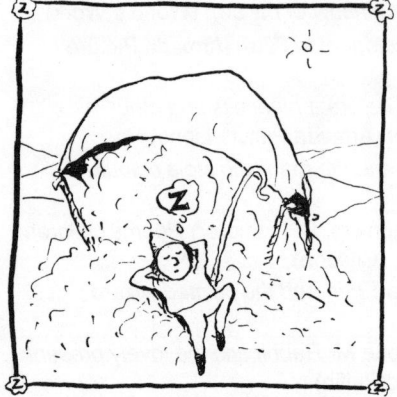

THEME
Mice

Session 1

Display books about mice; include fiction, picture story books and non-fiction titles (see bibliography).
Permit a browsing time to allow children to acquaint themselves with mice characters.

Read one of the stories from the display, for example, *Once a mouse* by Brown.

Activity

Write the name of a mouse character, the title of the story, the author's and the illustrator's names, on to prepared mouse shapes.
Use these mouse shapes as a wall display, or make them into a mobile.

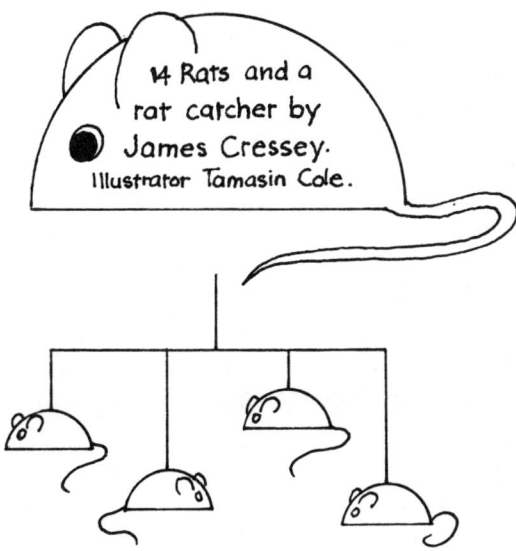

Session 2

Read 'Mice' by Rose Fyleman in *Time for poetry*.

Session 3

Read *Geraldine the music mouse* by Lionni or *Frederick* by Lionni.

Activity

Make mouse shapes in Lionni style.
Have prepared shapes for the body, ears, eye-pieces and tail. These may become stick puppets for puppet plays about mice.

Discuss

Why do some people dislike mice?
Why is the cat the mouse's enemy?
Can you imagine a time when the cat and the mouse were friends?

Session 4

Story-telling

Follow up the discussion of a mouse and a cat being friends, with a telling of Aesop's fable 'Lion and the mouse'.

Discuss

Bravery and strength are attributes not only of the big.
In what other situations might a mouse have been able to help the lion?
Retell the story but tell what the ending may have been had the mouse *not* come to help the lion.

Session 5

Read *John the mouse who learned to read* by Randall.

Activity

Following the reading of the story have a cheese-tasting. This may be a 'literary luncheon' for the class. Eat cheese and biscuits while listening to stories and poems about mice.

Session 6

Read *Amos and Boris* by Steig.

Activities

Write a story about a mouse or an acrostic for the word 'mouse'.
  Mice creep
  Over and
  Under
  Stairways
  Everywhere

Display the children's writings with earlier displayed mouse poems and shapes containing names of mouse characters.

Session 7

Introduce the 'church mice' series by Oakley.
Read *The church mouse.*

Activities

Compile a 'mouse menu'. List breakfast, lunch and dinner foods for a mouse family.

Establish a 'mouse house'.
Keep mice as pets in the library or classroom.
They are quite delightful if the cage is kept clean.
Note: Mice should not be fed too much cheese. They are happier with grain foods.

Bibliography

Arbuthnot, May Hill *Time for poetry* (Scott Forseman)
Brown, M. *Once a mouse* (Atheneum)
Carle, E. *Do you want to be my friend*? (Harper & Row)
Gag, W. *Snippy and Snappy* (Faber)
Lionni, L. *Frederick* (Abelard-Schuman/Armada Picture Lions)
—— *Geraldine the music mouse* (Andersen)
Lobel, A. *Mouse soup* (World's Work)
—— *Mouse tales* (World's Work)
Moore, Inga *Aktil's bicycle ride* (Oxford University Press)
Oakley, G. *The church mouse* (Macmillan)
Steig, W. *Amos and Boris* (Puffin)
Thomas, U. *Apple-mouse* (Angus & Robertson)
Yeoman, M. and Blake, Q. *Mouse trouble* (Puffin)

THEME
Bears

Session 1

Tell the story of 'Goldilocks and the three bears'.

Activity

Display factual books and pictures of real bears along with picture-books and fiction material about bears.
Allow the children time to browse.

Discuss

What different types of bears do we know?
Are all bears the same?
Are the bears in Goldilocks like any real bears?
Where do bears live?

Activity

Make a mural of the setting for 'Goldilocks and the three bears'.
Perhaps work could begin on a box construction of the bears' house.

Session 2

Read *A kiss for Little Bear* by Minarik.

Discuss

Talk about the sequence of the animals as the kiss is passed back to Little Bear.
How did you feel while you were listening to the story?
Does Little Bear like his grandmother?
How do you know this from the story?

Activities

Draw a picture that you would like to send to your grandmother.

Introduce the series of books about Little Bear.
Display these to encourage borrowing for personal reading.

Session 3

Tell *The story of Horace* by Coates.
As the story progresses invite the audience to respond with the phrases:
   What do you think has happened?
   What has happened?
   Horace has eaten _____.
   I will kill that Horace.

Discuss

Discuss the relationships and sequence of generations in Horace's family.
Make a diagram to illustrate their 'family tree'.

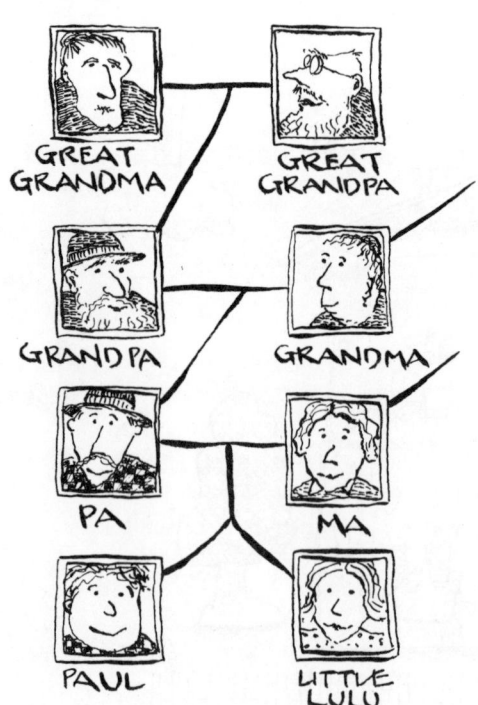

14

Activity

Use the prepared outline shapes on page 17 to draw the characters. Enlarge them using an overhead projector and assign a group of students the task of colouring, using waxcrayon, paint or pastel, one of the characters.
These 'larger than life' characters may be used during future telling sessions.
Each character is removed as Horace eats.

Session 4

Tell 'The Bear with One Eye' in *Three bags full* by Ainsworth.

Activity

Act out the story with individual children or groups of children saying the words said by the bead box, the work basket, the plasticine, etc.

Make stick puppets for each of the characters to use in future retellings.
The orders could be on signs for use too.

Session 5

Activity

Participation story — 'Going on a bear hunt'.
Try this variation on the lion hunt in *Juba this and Juba that* by Tashjian or in *Three bags full* by Ainsworth.
Teacher and children sit in a semi-circle.
T. Would you like to go on a bear hunt?
C. Yes, we would.
Children repeat everything the teacher does and everything the teacher says.
T. Let's start.
T. It's early morning and we'll jump out of bed. Have a big stretch.
The 'hunt' can be as long or as short as time permits by adding actions to the sequence:
    Walk over the bridge.
    Ride some of the way on horseback.
    Jump the river.
    Get caught in sloshy mud,
    attacked by biting mosquitoes etc.

Session 6

Read Selected poetry — 'Furry Bear' by A. A. Milne in *A children's zoo* and 'Bear in There' by Silverstein in *A light in the attic*.

Discuss

Where do the bears live?
What do they both like about the place?
What do they have to keep them warm?
Draw attention to Milne's use of nonsense words, 'snew' and 'fiz'.
Which poem do you think is the funniest? Why?

Session 7

Finish this unit by holding a 'Teddy bears' picnic' or morning tea. Invite all of the students to bring their favourite stuffed toy and a plate of its favourite food.
Share food and toys.
Read more bear stories.

Bibliography

Ainsworth, Ruth *Three bags full* (Heinemann)

Coates, A. *The story of Horace* (Faber)

—— *The bears on Hemlock Mountain* (Puffin)

Flack, M. *Ask Mr Bear* (Macmillan)

Gretz, Susanna *Teddybears 1 to 10* (Benn/Armada Picture Lions)

—— *The bears who went to the seaside* (Benn/Puffin)

—— *The bears who stayed indoors* (Benn/Puffin)

Kraus, R. *Milton the early riser* (Hamish Hamilton)

Lobel, Arnold *Bears in the air* (World's Work)

Minarik, E. H. *Little Bear* (series) (World's Work)

Moss, E. and Baker, J. *Polar* (Puffin)

Peet, Bill *Big bad Bruce* (Deutsch)

Silverstein, Shel *A light in the attic* (Harper & Row)

Tashjian, Virginia *Juba this and Juba that* (Little, Brown)

Watson, Julia (compiler) *A children's zoo* (Fontana Lion)

Reproducible page — Bears

The story of Horace

Outline drawings of the characters to enable teacher to enlarge on OHP for display and life size puppets. These drawings may also be used for finger puppets.

PICTURE STORY BOOKS

Books by one author

Introduce the works of one author.
Authors appropriate for this level include:
Beatrix Potter
Pat Hutchins
Roger Duvoisin
Edward Ardizzone
Arnold Lobel
Brian Wildsmith
Ezra Jack Keats

Session 1

Activity

Display all of the books by the author you
have chosen to feature.
Allow a browsing time for children to
become familiar with the author's choice of
topics and characters.

Discuss

What types of things does this author write
about? For example, Beatrix Potter writes
mostly about animals. Encourage
individual students to tell something about
the book they were looking at during the
browsing time. Does this author draw
his/her own pictures?
Talk about the role of an author, and the
role of an illustrator.

Read one of the stories by the chosen
author.

Session 2

Read the first page of the selected story.
Stop and ask children to predict what
might happen.
Reassess predictions at the half-way point.
After the reading, discuss the predictions
made.

Discuss

Discuss the characters and setting of the
story.

Look at the illustrations and encourage
children to recognize the technique used
by the illustrator, for example, line drawing,
painting, collage, photographs.
Compare this book's illustrations with
those of the book in the previous session.
Choose a favourite illustration from the
book and discuss the colours used. Look
for detail in the illustration to highlight the
point that, in a picture story book, the
illustrations carry detail to release the
author from the need to write long
descriptive passages. For example, in
Peter Rabbit by Potter, Mr McGregor has a
hedge as a fence. There is a forest close
to his farm yard. The illustrator shows us
what Farmer McGregor wears while he is
working.
Encourage the students to verbalize the
stories told by the illustrations.

Note: It is not the authors' intention that the study of an illustrator's style become the subject of detailed and tedious analysis. The mood of these discussions should, as with all discussion sessions about literature, be relaxed, supportive and friendly: a sharing of thoughts and impressions.

Session 3

Read another story by the chosen author. Have children retell the story using the illustrations as a guide to sequence, setting and plot.

Discuss

If applicable, compare the illustrator's style with the approach used in earlier works by the author, and discuss the differences.

Session 4

Read another story by the author.

Activities

Complete a worksheet similar to any one of the following.

Pat Hutchins wrote a book called Rosie's walk.

Rosie the hen went for a walk.

Pat Hutchins is an author.

Edward Ardizzone wrote stories about Tim.

Here is Tim and his friend Ginger.

Edward Ardizzone drew the pictures too.

Arnold Lobel is an author and an illustrator. He made up a story called Giant John.

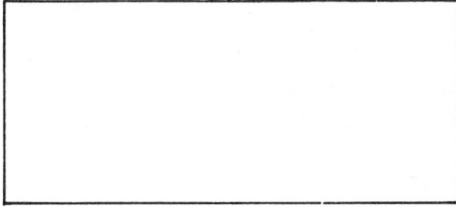_____ is a silly goose

Petunia

The author is Roger Duvoisin and he drew the pictures too.

- Keep reading the author's works.
- Write a letter to the author/illustrator. Detail the impressions and thoughts of the group now that the study is complete.
- Make a mural containing all of the characters created by the author.
- Discuss the similarities/differences in the author's stories.
- Make up alternative titles for each of the stories.

PICTURE STORY BOOKS

Single picture-book activities

Read *Millions of cats* by Gagg.

Discuss

Where and when did the story take place?
How do you know it was a long time ago?
(Look at costumes in illustrations.)

Activity

Draw a 'million' cats.
Each child draws and cuts out a cardboard cat.
Display and attach caption

  Hundreds of cats

  Thousands of cats

  Millions and billions and trillions of cats

Read *Meg and Mog* by Nicholl.

Discuss

How would you describe Meg and Mog?
Make a list of descriptive words.
Add words to describe witches other than Meg.
Encourage children to tell about other witches that they know. What are they like?

Activity

Draw, paint or construct cut-out shapes of the main characters.

Read more of the Meg stories.

Read *The lighthouse keeper's lunch* by Armitage.

Discuss

What were the three ways that Mrs Grinling tried to trick the seagulls?
Which one worked? Would you like to be a lighthouse keeper?
What jobs would you have to do each day?
How would you get across to Mr Grinling's lighthouse if the sea was too dangerous for the boat?

Activity

Make up a lunch menu that you would send down the wire.
Draw and cut out seagulls to complete a display constructed by the teacher. This display could include a large cut-out lighthouse, the sea, the small white cottage and the basket slipping down the rope.

Read *Peter and Roland* by Graham.

Discuss

How did Peter care for the budgie?

How do you think Peter felt when the budgie flew away?
Where did he look?
Do you think the budgie was happier with Peter or the racing pigeons? Why?

Activity

Make a list of all the things the budgie did in Peter's house.
Think of a name for the budgie.
Draw large pictures of the budgie, cut them out and place round the classroom. Label with chosen names.

Picture-books about one character

Introduce a series of books about one character, for example, Harry, in Gene Zion's *Harry the dirty dog*.

Session 1

Read *Harry the dirty dog*.

Discuss

How did Harry get dirty.
Why did he hide the brush?
Why don't dogs enjoy baths?
Does your dog like to be bathed?

Activity

Draw and cut out shapes of Harry.
Draw a picture of all the places that Harry visited. Arrange them in sequence on a display board.
Some will show Harry the dirty dog and some will show him clean.
Begin an individual booklet for each child.

Session 2

Read *Harry by the sea*.

Discuss

In *Harry the dirty dog*, Harry is not recognized because he gets dirty. What is his disguise this time?
How do people feel when they see Harry under the seaweed?
Harry is lost. Why?
Have you ever been lost?
Who causes Harry to lose his disguise?
Why was the new umbrella easy for Harry to find?
How else could Harry's family have made it easy for him to find them?

Activity

Add to the pages of individual booklets about Harry.
Make a wall picture of the beach. (Each child cuts out an umbrella shape.)

Session 3

Read *No roses for Harry*.

Discuss

What presents have you been given that you have disliked?
What clothes don't you like to wear?

Harry has had three different appearances so far:
1 dirt   2 seaweed   3 sweater
Try to think of another way that Harry might be disguised.
Make up a story about it.

Activity

List or draw the ways Harry tries to get rid of his sweater.

Session 4

Read *Harry and the lady next door.*

Other characters appearing in a series of books:
Petunia by Duvoisin (goose)
Frog and Toad by Lobel (frog)
Little Bear by Minarik (bear)
Captain Pugwash by Ryan (pirate)

NURSERY RHYMES

Session 1

Introduce the unit with a 'Who am I?' quiz.
For example:
> I sat on a wall.
> I had a fall.
> The soldiers couldn't help me, who am I?

As each character is identified, sing the nursery rhyme.
Read nursery rhymes as a shared book using *Time for a rhyme* (Nelson).

Activities

As the group sings selected rhymes, some children perform actions appropriate for characters and situations described.

Plan a grand occasion.
Children dress up and act out nursery rhymes in outdoor settings.
Film/video the production.
Re-play to the accompaniment of the class singing the nursery rhyme.
Some percussion work could be included.
Film the 'choir' and 'orchestra' so that everyone is in the picture.

Session 2

Activity

Compile a nursery rhyme collection.
Each child draws a picture of their favourite nursery rhyme character.

Talk about clothing for the character and where the action takes place.

Collect the pictures and type the nursery rhymes to accompany them.

Sing and introduce some percussion instrument work.

Session 3

Activity

Play 'Who am I'.
Children mime the actions of a nursery rhyme character; the rest of the class guess who it is.

Many children should be able to write 'Who am I?' clues.
Work the children in groups of two or three to assist less able writers.
Make 'Who Am I?' cards.

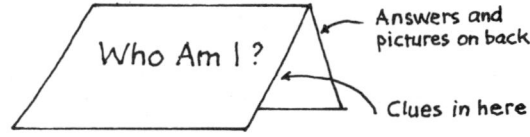

Use these for future quiz games. Authors read their cards to the class.

Session 4

Puzzle pages (see pp. 24–25)

What's wrong here?

Old mother Hubbard
Went to the cupboard
To get her poor dog a bone.

Little Boy Blue
Come blow your horn
The sheep's in the meadow
The cow's in the corn.

Hey diddle diddle
The cat and the fiddle
The cow jumped over
the moon.

Sing a song of sixpence
A pocket full of rye
Four and twenty black birds
Baked in a pie.

Cut and paste to put these mixed-up nursery rhymes in order.

Name: _____

Old King Cole was a | old | merry

soul

Dumpty | Humpty | had a great fall

Jack and Jill | up the hill | went

Miss | Little | Muffet | on her tuffet

sat

FAIRY TALES

Session 1

Activity

Make a display of characters from fairy tales which have events taking place in threes.

Using the display, ask children to identify the fairy tale to which each character belongs.

Tell 'The three billy goats gruff'.
Try to modify your voice to fit each goat.

Discuss

What problem did the goats have to overcome?
How did they solve this problem?

Activities

Make word lists to describe the troll and the goats.

Draw the troll; remember to include the details mentioned in the story.

Dramatize the tale.

Session 2

Read *The three billy goats gruff* by Galdone.

Discuss

Compare the book-reading with the previous retelling.
Do they differ in any way?
What phrases are repeated?
Compare Galdone's drawing of the troll with the children's drawings, emphasizing that each drawing is different because each of us has a different approach to art.
Note: Galdone has illustrated other fairy tales.
Ashton Scholastic has published a large book edition of this tale.

Activity

Use the reproducible page to place the characters in the correct sequence. (See p. 28.)

Session 3

Tell 'Goldilocks and the three bears'.

Discuss

What were the three things that Goldilocks did?
What phrases are repeated by the bears?
Which of the bears do you think suffered most? Why?
Note: For older children, read *Revolting rhymes* by R. Dahl.

Activity

Draw each bear's chair, porridge bowl and bed using paper appropriate to the *size* of each bear, e.g. three small sheets of paper for the little bear's chair, bowl and bed. Mount these drawings on card, laminate and cut up into jigsaws.

Session 4

Tell 'The three little pigs'.

Discuss

Describe each character. Ask children to demonstrate how they feel each character would talk.
What phrases are repeated?
Outline the sequence of main events.

Activity

Make puppets for each character using details outlined in the 'Colour' theme. (Alternately children could make paper-bag masks.)
Use these puppets to dramatize the story.

Follow up by reading or telling other fairy tales about animals, e.g. 'The wolf and the seven little kids' and 'Little Red Riding Hood'.

Compile a theme about female characters in fairy tales, e.g. Cinderella, Snow White, Rapunzel or Sleeping Beauty.

Cut each of the boxes out and place them in the correct sequence.

Level 2 Ages 8–9

Framework for Ages 8–9 literature program

Activities

Themes
    Magical and mythical beasts
    Dragons
    Giants
    Circus
    Pirates
    Cats
    Dogs
Picture story books
    Single picture-book activities
Book studies — Fiction
    The golden bird by Edith Brill
    Greensmoke by Rosemary Manning
    The Iron Man by Ted Hughes

Framework for Age 8 literature program

Abilities to be reached	Teaching points	Literary forms appropriate for level
Distinguish between picture story, fiction and factual books.	Using a particular theme, e.g. cats, compare books from each category.	Picture story Poetry
Verbalize obvious themes in fiction books.	What is the main idea behind the story?	Story-telling Nursery rhymes
Verbalize sequence of main events in a fiction book and identify the story's climax.	Children retell the story and identify the most exciting part. Discuss what events led up to the climax.	Short stories Simple fiction
Predict outcome of the plot, for a particular fiction book.	Occasionally stop reading prior to completion of story and discuss possible outcomes.	Fables
Identify main character of a fiction book and describe chief physical features.	Children compile simple word lists to describe characters. Draw characters and list words that describe them; make a display of this.	
Describe contribution of illustrations in developing a particular setting.	What do we learn about the setting from the illustrations? Children illustrate their ideas for a given setting, e.g. desert, underwater; then read a story for that setting.	
Identify strong emotion in a simple fiction book.	How did the character feel when . . . ? What words did the author use to portray this feeling?	

Framework for Age 9 literature program

Abilities to be reached	Teaching points	Literary forms appropriate for level
Distinguish between poetry, prose, and drama; explain differences.	Read selections from each type and discuss basic differences in writing style; display examples of each. Children use a particular theme to write extracts in each of these three styles.	Picture story Poetry Story-telling Short story collections
Identify the theme of a particular novel and relate to real life.	Relate theme, through discussion, to children's own experiences. Discuss particular social problems raised in the story, e.g. conservation in *Dinosaurs and all that rubbish*.	Fiction (fantasy, humour, realism) Drama Fables
Explain the contribution of illustrations in developing the sequence of main events and climax of a particular novel.	Children sequence events through illustrations, in comic strip/story-board format. Introduce no-text picture story books, such as those by Mordillo, as a means of demonstrating this approach.	Folk tales
Identify from a chosen novel the main character's strengths and weaknesses.	Use discussion, role-playing and dramatization of events with this ability.	
Predict what the main character will do after the story has ended.	What did the main character do after the story ended? Were you satisfied with the ending? Write a plot outline for a possible sequel.	
Describe the contribution of an illustrator in developing a particular setting.	What did we learn about the setting from the illustrations? What art techniques have been used by the illustrator? Children illustrate their ideas for a given setting.	
Identify the motivation for a particular character's action.	Why did the character act as he or she did? What would you have done?	

THEME
Magical and mythical beasts

Session 1

Introduce stories about unicorns, dragons, bunyips, glerps (see bibliography).
List all of those known by the children and discuss the appearance and behaviour of the creatures.
Read a story selected from the bibliography.

Activity

Illustrate the story read, or your favourite story about a magical or mythical creature.

Session 2

Create a make-believe creature.

Write a description of the creature's physical appearance, behaviour and environment under the following headings:
    What it looks like
    What it eats
    Where it lives
    How it moves
    What it does
    How it sounds
Read a story selected from the bibliography.

Session 3

Make an illustrated poster of the creature and attach the written description.
Display these posters with books about beasts and creatures.

Session 4

Activities

Tell the story of 'The Hobyahs' retold in *Juba this and Juba that* by Tashjian.

How can you calm down an angry dragon? Throw water on him and he will let off steam.
Why do dragons sleep during the day? So they can fight nights (knights).

Sing 'Puff the magic dragon' and 'The spangled pandemonium'.

Make a jig-saw puzzle.
Paste an illustration of a favourite creature on to heavy card; don't make this too small. Laminate or cover with Contact or Duraseal. Cut the board into jig-saw pieces.

Session 5

How many words can you make using the letters from the word 'dragon'?
ran   go   Dan   drag   nod   rag
do   Don   road   God   dog   and
many more.

Make this a poetry reading session using selections from *Milliganimals* by Milligan and *Prefabulous animiles* by Reeves.

Teacher copies favourite poems on to display charts; children illustrate each chart.

Encourage children to learn their favourite verse and recite it for the class.

Session 6

Read a story selected from the bibliography and children's writings from Session 2.

Activities

Prepare a story sequence chart for the story,
    or
make cut-out of characters from the story for a mobile,
    or
retell the story using percussion instruments as a sound score.

Session 7

Read a story selected from the bibliography.

Activity

Discuss and make a list of all magical animals/monsters read about and discussed so far.
Arrange in alphabetical order.
Classify the creatures under the following headings.
    Good/Bad
    Real/Imaginary
    Humorous/Scarey

Session 8

Read a story selected from the bibliography.

Discuss

Where do the creatures live?

Activity

List the habitats or settings of stories, e.g.
    Hobyahs — forest, caves
    Bunyips — swamps
    Dragons — caves
    Unicorns — mountains

33

Bibliography

Balian, L. *The animal* (Abingdon)

Dugan, Michael *Dragon's breath* (Puffin)

Kahl, V. *How do you hide a monster* (Scribner)

Klein, Robin *Thing* (Oxford University Press)

Mayer, M. *One monster after another* (Dial)

——— *There's a nightmare in my closet* (Dial)

Milligan, Spike *Milliganimals* (Puffin)

Niland, Deborah *A. B. C. of monsters* (Hodder)

Pavey, Peter *One dragon's dream* (Nelson/Puffin)

Peet, Bill *Cyrus the unsinkable sea serpent* (Deutsch)

Reeves, James *Prefabulous animiles* (Heinemann)

Roughsey, Dick *Giant devil dingo* (Collins)

Sage, A. and Calvi, G. *The ogre's banquet* (Doubleday)

Sendak, Maurice *Where the wild things are* (Bodley Head/Puffin)

Stern, S. *The Hobyahs* (Magnet Books/Methuen)

Tashjian, Virginia *Juba this and Juba that* (Little, Brown)

Wagner, Jenny *The bunyip of Berkeley's Creek* (Puffin)

THEME
Dragons

Session 1

Read or tell 'Stan Bolovan' in *A book of dragons* by Manning-Sanders.

Discuss

Briefly discuss children's feelings about the story.
Lead discussion to consider main characters and sequence of events.
Examine the way in which exaggeration provides humour.

Activities

Children construct wall frieze of events.
Role-play emotions of characters: wife/unhappy; Stan/bold; dragon/fearful.

Session 2

Read *A dragon in the clockbox* by Craig.

Discuss

What secrets or make-believe characters did you have when you were younger?
Do you know of others who have secret friends?
Compare this character with those in the previous story.

Activities

Illustrate the 'life cycle' of a dragon.

A lion in the meadow by Mahy is a related story.

Session 3

Read *Custard the dragon* and 'The toaster' by Nash.

Discuss

Compare literary form used here with previous forms.

Activities

List words used to describe the dragons.
Classify these into three groups:
    What they look like
    What they do
    How they sound
Use this word list as a resource for children's writing about dragons, whether in prose or verse format.

Session 4

Read *Droofus the dragon* by Peet.

Discuss

What do the illustrations contribute, in relation to setting? Compare this setting with those of previous stories.

Activities

Illustrate your idea for the setting of a

dragon story. Read *One dragon's dream* by Pavey to further explore the role of illustrations in establishing setting.

Session 5

Read a story from the bibliography.

Discuss

Focus on motivation for actions; why did the character act as he or she did?
What would you have done in the same circumstances?
Consider points raised in earlier sessions, i.e. plot, characters, setting.
Aim to summarize abilities and activities treated so far, prior to Session 6.

Session 6

Introduce *Greensmoke* by Manning.
It is suggested that this story be serialized. Read *daily* to your class and, where appropriate, include follow-up activities similar to those suggested earlier.
For a detailed study of *Greensmoke* see page 66.

Bibliography

Baumann, H. *Dragon mountain* (Dent)

Bradfield, R. *A good knight for dragons* (World's Work)

Cole, T. *The dragon and George* (Black)

Craig, J. *The dragon in the clockbox* (World's Work)

DePaola, T. *The knight and the dragon* (Putnam)

Domanska, J. *King Krakus and the dragon* (Julia MacRae)

Drew, P. *Dream dragon* (Chatto)

Dugan, M. *Dragon's breath* (Puffin)

Kahl, V. *How many dragons are behind the door?* (Scribner)

Kingman, L. *Georgina the dragon* (Archway)

Konopka, U. *George the dragon* (Dent)

McNaughton, C. *King Nonn the wiser* (Heinemann)

Mahy, M. *A lion in the meadow* (Dent/Puffin)

—— *The dragon of an ordinary family* (Heinemann)

Manning-Sanders, R. *A book of dragons* (Methuen)

Nash, O. *Custard the dragon* (Warne)

—— 'The toaster' (poem)

Pavey, P. *One dragon's dream* (Nelson/Puffin)

Peet, B. *Cyrus the unsinkable sea serpent* (Deutsch)

—— *How Droofus the dragon lost his head* (Deutsch)

Van Woerkom, D. *Alexandra the rock eater* (Knopf)

THEME
Giants

Session 1

Read *Giant John* by Lobel.

Discuss

How does the plot develop in *Giant John*?
List the jobs done by the giant.
What other jobs would a giant be good at
doing?

Activity

Draw the jobs that Giant John did at the
castle.
Arrange these pictures in sequence.

Play 'Musical chairs'. Relate this game to
those parts of the story where John
danced to the fairies' magic music; he
could not stop until the music stopped.

Session 2

Read *The selfish giant* by Wilde.

Discuss

What is selfishness?
How did the giant show his selfishness?
What is the opposite of selfishness?
How was the giant punished for his
selfishness?
What did the children do to cause the giant
to change?
What happened as the giant grew old?
What are the effects of old age?

Activity

Draw four pictures to show
the giant's garden at
different times in the story.

Session 3

Read 'The brave little tailor' in *A book of giants* by Manning-Sanders.

Discuss

Talk about the bravery of the tailor.
Why did people believe that he was brave?
Was he brave?
How did he trick the giants?
What makes a brave person?
Describe a brave person you know.
What other ways could you have tricked the giants?

Activity

Draw the tailor tricking the giants.

Write a sentence or sentences about the tailor. Imagine that you are a reporter writing about the tailor's bravery for a newspaper or television news broadcast.

Session 4

Read 'The little boy's secret' by Harrison in *The book of giant stories*.

Discuss

Compare the giants that have been introduced in the sessions so far.
Which ones were friendly? funny? dangerous?

Activity

List words to describe giants.
Classify these words into sounds of a giant, giant's movements, physical appearance, moods of a giant.

Draw a picture of each giant.
Make a 'Rogue's gallery of giants'.

Session 5

Read 'Me and my giant' by Shel Silverstein in *Giant poems*; 'Like a giant in a towel' by Dennis Lee in *Giant poems*; and 'Big little boy' by Eve Merriam in *Poems children will sit still for*.

Discuss

Compare the effectiveness of this literary form in depicting giants, with the prose form heard in previous sessions.

Activities

Compile a list of comparisons between giants and small things.

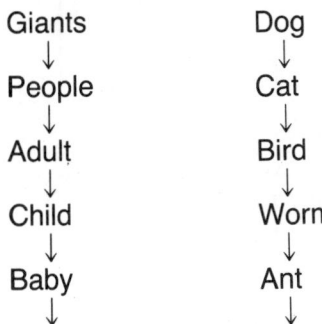

Giants	Dog
↓	↓
People	Cat
↓	↓
Adult	Bird
↓	↓
Child	Worm
↓	↓
Baby	Ant
↓	↓

Write sentences about the comparisons, e.g.

    A dog is a giant to a flea.
    A tree is a giant to a flower.

Make up a 'giant' story. Write it on a 'giant' piece of paper, using large print. Refer to the word lists compiled in Session 4.

Session 6

Tell 'Jack and the beanstalk'.

Activity

Complete sequencing activity using the reproducible on p. 41. (In a future session introduce *Jim and the beanstalk* by Briggs.)

Session 7

Tell 'David and Goliath' in 1 Samuel 17.

Discuss

Bravery is not dependent on a person's size.
Talk about giants from earlier times, e.g. Atlas, Cyclops.
Complete the giant's crossword p. 40.

Bibliography

Briggs, Raymond *Jim and the beanstalk* (Puffin)
Carle, Eric *Watchout! A giant* (Hamilton)
Harrison, David L. *The book of giant stories* (Cape)
Herrmann, F. *Giant Alexander* (Methuen/Puffin)
Lobel, Arnold *Giant John* (World's Work/Puffin)
Manning-Sanders, Ruth *A book of giants* (Methuen)
Silverstein, Shel *Where the sidewalk ends* (Harper & Row)
Wallace, D. *Giant poems* (Holiday House)
Wilde, Oscar *The selfish giant* (Evans)

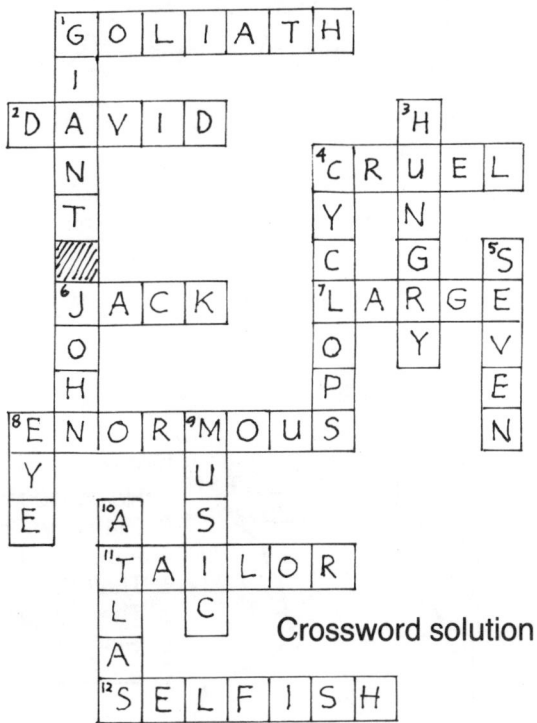

Crossword solution

A giant crossword

Across

1 David and _____.
2 _____ and Goliath.
4 Giants are often mean and _____.
6 _____ and the beanstalk.
7 A giant has _____ hands and feet
8 Means very big.
11 The brave little _____.
12 The _____ giant.

Down

1 He danced when the fairies played their music.
3 Giants are always _____ and want food.
4 A giant with only one eye.
5 The brave little tailor said, "I killed _____ in one blow."
8 The cyclops only has one of these.
9 Giant John danced to the _____ played by the fairies.
10 _____ held up the world on his shoulders.

Draw a picture for each part of the story of 'Jack and the beanstalk'. Cut up the illustration to make a book with 9 pages.

'Fee Fi Fo Fum', the giant comes home.

Jack steals the giant's gold.

Jack climbs to the giant's house.

Jack takes the hen that lays the golden eggs.

Jack exchanges the cow for the magic beans.

Jack steals the magic harp.

Beanstalk grows and reaches the sky.

Giant chases Jack down the beanstalk. Jack chops the beanstalk.

Giant's wife hides Jack.

THEME
Circus

This unit of work for all levels incorporates language, art, music and literature activities.

Choose books from the bibliography which you feel are suitable for your children's interests and abilities.

Introduce, read and discuss these books over several sessions and, where appropriate, include an activity from the following section.

Brief book reports could be displayed with the books, the art work, and other written material produced during the theme's treatment. See p. 114 for ideas on book report writing.

Activities

Introduce this activity by displaying and discussing alphabet and counting books. Make an alphabet book. Assign each student a letter of the alphabet and have them illustrate the theme.

For example: **A A**crobat
B Bears
C Clowns

Extend captioning to phrases or sentences.

Agile **a**rialists swing high above.

Make a counting book.

For example: **1 One** ringmaster
2 Two trapeze artists
3 Three trotting ponies

Combine counting and the alphabet in one book.

For example: **Eleven l**eaping **l**ions
Seven capering **c**lowns

List all items associated with the circus. Draw a circus ring and label the objects in the ring with words from the list. This could be done individually or as a group wall frieze for a display area.

List all the describing words for one type of performer, for example, clowns, acrobats, lion-tamer.

Use these words to compose poetry, descriptive paragraphs or short stories about a particular person belonging to a circus troupe.

Acrostic writing (suitable for all grades)
C lowning
I nteresting
R ing master
C lapping and cheering
U nder the big top
S ensational

Poetry

Read 'The circus', by C. J. Dennis in *Chosen for children* (Angus & Robertson); 'The circus parade' in *Time for poetry* (Scott Foresman); *'Circus'* by Margaret Stanley-Wrench in *Rhyme and rhythm* (Yellow Book) (Macmillan).

Discuss

What is the mood of the poems? How has the poet created the excitement of the circus?

Activities

Have the poems copied on to large charts and illustrated for display.
Encourage individuals and groups to say these poems aloud. Make poetry cards; have copies available for borrowing by the children.
Encourage individuals to compile their own poetry card sets.

Mime the actions for a particular circus personality. Individuals or small groups may be involved in role-playing using the cards provided on p. 45.

Play '20 questions' or 'Secret word', using the following instructions.
'20 questions'
One player writes down on a slip of paper, a description of a circus performer, animal or circus act.
The remaining players have 20 questions to guess what has been written on the paper.
The questions must be framed so as to be answered with only 'yes' or 'no'.

'Secret word'
Divide the class into two groups.

A player from one team leaves the room. The rest of the team are shown the secret word.
When their team-mate returns to the room, the team has one minute to give one word clues for the secret word. For example, if the secret word is 'Ring-master', clues might be 'man, boss, organizer, announcer, etc.'

Listen to 'The comedians' from *The dance of the comedians* by Smetana. Link this music with the story, *Joey the clown* by D. B. Kabalevsky.

Record the soundtrack for a circus performance. Use music with students reading their own descriptions of the acts; make sound effects of the crowd, animals, and performers.

Make clown masks, clown puppets.
Paint the windows of your classroom. A different circus act could be featured in each pane.
Cut silhouettes of circus animals and performers.

Draw a series of illustrations to record the sequence of a particular circus act.
For example:

Arrange these pictures into a zig-zag display sheet.

Students use grease paint to devise a clown make-up for a friend or for themselves.

Design a circus poster: a simple design for junior students; more detail for senior students. Include time, place, cost, dates, and information.

Try balancing, tumbling or human pyramids.

Bibliography

Abels, Harriet Sheffer *The circus detectives* (Cheshire)

Anno *Dr Anno's magical midnight circus* (Weatherbill)

Bissett, Donald *Benjie the circus dog* (Benn)

Bond, Michael *Paddington at the circus* (Collins)

Clewes, Dorothy *Upside down Willie* (Hamish Hamilton)

Crowther, Carol *Clowns and clowning* (Macdonald)

Foster, Leslie *Circus maths* (Macdonald)

Greenwood, Ted *The pochetto coat* (Hutchinson)

Gunthorp, Karen *Millie at the circus* (Doubleday)

Hoff, Syd *Julius* (World's Work)

Hornby, John *Clowns through the ages* (Oliver & Boyd)

Huber, Ursula *The Nock Family Circus* (Benn)

Jacobs, Allan D. *Behind the circus tent* (Lerner)

Jenkins, Alan C. *Circuses through the ages* (Chatto & Boyd)

Kabalevsky, D. B. *Joey the clown* (Gakken)

Kastner, Erich *The little man* (Penguin)

Lindgren, Astrid *Circus child* (Methuen)

Lofting, Hugh *Dr. Dolittle's circus* (Jonathan Cape)

Long, Ruthanna *The runaway circus* (Golden Press)

Pearce, Margaret *The circus runaways* (Penguin)

Prelutsky, J. *Circus* (Hamish Hamilton)

Ramsbottom, Edward *The circus* (Macmillan)

Sanchez, J. L. Garcia *I am a circus* (Blackwell)

Webb, Anne *Circus* (Blackwell)

Wildsmith, Brian *The circus* (Oxford University Press)

Role-playing cards

Reproducible page
Photocopy, place on card for use by children

The liontamer

You are in a cage with five lions. You have a whip and you carry a long stick. Two lions are on a plank above you. The other lions are reluctant to leave their pedestals. How will you make them join the others on the plank?

The ringmaster

You have a large moustache. You hold a microphone and you announce the tightrope walker. Describe the act, anticipating a possible fall. There is no safety net.

The clown

You are wearing enormous shoes. You carry a bucket and threaten to throw its contents over the members of the audience. Your trousers keep falling down every time you swing the bucket. How do you keep your trousers up?

The tightrope walker

You are on the ledge ready to walk on to the wire. You hold a long pole for balance. Walk to the middle of the rope, turn around, pretend to stumble. Put down the pole and skip with a rope which was tied around your waist.

The trapeze artist

You climb the ladder to the ledge high above. When you reach it you prepare to swing out as the catcher. You prepare your hands and feet to ensure a good grip. Count to four before swinging out for the catch.

A person in the audience

You are a little boy/girl. You are eating a large ice-cream. You are watching the trapeze act. Your ice-cream melts and drips down your hand. As you try to take out your handkerchief to wipe your hand, you drop your ice-cream.

Reproducible page

Find the hidden words that describe the circus.
- Things
- Feelings
- Actions

There are 20 hidden words.

A	B	E	N	T	E	R	T	A	I	N	I	N	G	C	D	E	F
G	H	I	J	U	K	L	M	A	N	I	M	A	L	S	N	X	O
P	Q	R	S	M	T	U	V	W	T	X	Y	Z	A	B	C	C	D
B	E	F	G	B	H	I	J	P	R	A	N	C	I	N	G	I	K
A	L	M	N	L	O	A	C	R	O	B	A	T	I	C	P	T	Q
L	R	S	F	I	S	A	W	-	D	U	S	T	T	U	V	E	W
A	X	C	A	N	V	A	S	X	U	Y	Z	A	B	C	D	M	T
N	E	L	N	G	F	G	O	R	C	H	E	S	T	R	A	E	R
C	H	O	F	I	J	A	U	D	I	E	N	C	E	K	P	N	A
I	L	W	A	M	N	O	P	Q	N	R	S	T	U	V	P	T	I
N	W	N	R	X	Y	Z	B	I	G	-	T	O	P	A	L	B	N
G	C	S	E	D	E	F	G	H	I	J	K	P	A	R	A	D	E
L	M	N	O	P	Q	R	S	T	U	V	W	X	Y	Z	U	A	R
B	C	P	E	R	F	O	R	M	E	R	S	D	E	F	S	X	S
	G	H	I	J	K	L	M	N	O	P	Q	R	S	E	T	U	
	S	O	M	E	R	S	A	U	L	T	V	W	X	Y	Z	A	

46

THEME
Pirates

Session 1

Read *Captain Pugwash* by Ryan, or another selection from the bibliography.

Discuss

Talk about the meaning of the word 'pirate'.
How are the two pirates in *Captain Pugwash* different?

Activity

Draw a pirate or his ship, or make a pirate flag.

Session 2

Display all the pirate books you have collected for this theme.
After the children have browsed for five to ten minutes, invite them to tell about the books they have been reading.
Teacher can highlight different types of pirates — mean, funny, etc.

Discuss

Children and teacher talk about famous pirates — Long John Silver, Captain Blood, Blackbeard, Captain Hook (Peter Pan). Introduce books where appropriate. Compile lists of pirates' names.

Follow up by referring older children to *World book encyclopedia*, Macdonald topic book *Pirates* and others from the non-fiction titles listed in the bibliography. For juniors, introduce other *Pugwash* books and discuss the work of the author/illustrator John Ryan.

Session 3

Discuss

What do pirates look like? Using the material gathered and compiled in the previous sessions, children list words to describe a pirate.
Group these words according to appearance, behaviour, language, habitat.

Read 'The Pirate Don Durk of Dowdee', p. 322 in *Time for poetry*; 'The pirate's tea party', p. 470 in *A Book of 1000 poems*; 'Captain Hook', p. 18 in *Where the sidewalk ends.*
Add words from the poems to the above list. Give children a copy of the poems and let them illustrate; display results.

Activity

Pirates often used secret codes on their maps to keep their treasures safe. After children have solved the coded message supplied on page 51, let them devise their own codes.

Session 4

Read a story selected from the bibliography; follow up with riddles and games.

Riddles

Why did the pirate put a chicken where he buried the treasure?
Because X (eggs) marks the spot.

How do pirates get their clothes clean?
They throw them overboard and they wash ashore.

What's the difference between a blind man and a retired pirate?
The blind man cannot see to go, the retired pirate cannot go to sea.

Games

'Walk the Plank' game.
Draw a plank shape on the ground. Blindfold your friend and see who can walk the plank without falling off (p. 47 *See the sea* by Virginia Ferguson).

In small groups make a treasure map, or
use the enclosed dice game on page 52 to locate the treasure.

Session 5

Use words from the word lists to write class/group/individual pirate stories or poems.

Make next session a 'Dress-up day'. (See ideas for hats, weapons, costumes in *Pirates*, Macdonald Topic Book, p. 30.)

Session 6

Dress-up day
Select activities from any of the following:
Paint 'porthole' shapes or cut out black paper shapes and illustrate what may be seen from a porthole.

Arrange desks in a pirate ship shape. Use as a setting for a play.

Use building blocks for ship construction.

Make model ships (paper, matchbox, etc.) and race them on water.

Make 'pirate' food and have a feast: red rum cordial, etc.

Sing sea shanties.

For older children: Follow up with a discussion on 'land pirates', such as highwaymen and bushrangers.

Bibliography

Fiction

Barrie, J. M. *Peter Pan* (Hodder/Puffin)
Linklater, Eric *The pirates and the deep green sea* (Penguin)
Stevenson, R. L. *Treasure Island* (Methuen/Puffin)

Picture story books

Aitchison, Jane *The pirate's tale* (Penguin)
Cooney, Barbara *Dionysos and the pirates* (Doubleday)
Joslin, Sesyle *What do you say dear?* (Faber)
Loof, Jan *My Grandma is a pirate* (Black)
McNaughton, Colin *The pirates: the amazing adventures of Anton B. Stanton* (Benn)
Mahy, Margaret *The man whose mother was a pirate* (Dent)

Needle, Jan *Rottenteeth* (Deutsch)

Ryan, John *Pugwash and the ghost ship* (Bodley Head) (all the rest of the series)

Scarry, Richard *Great steamboat mystery* (Collins)

Non-fiction

Brading, Tilla *Pirates* (Macdonald Topic Books Series)

Ferguson, Virginia *See the sea* (McGraw Hill)

Hellsing, Lennart *The pirate book* (Benn)

Huffman, Tytus *Pirate treasure* (Macdonald)

Law, Felicia *Pirates* (Collins)

Martin, Silas *Pirates* (Macmillan Fact Finder Series)

—— *Pirates and buccaneers* (Macdonald)

—— *Pirates and highwaymen* (Oliver and Boyd)

Poetry

Arbuthnot, May Hill and Root, Shelton L. *Time for poetry* (Scott Forseman)

A book of 1000 poems (Evans)

Silverstein, Shel *Where the sidewalk ends* (Harper & Row)

Answers to pirates crossword page 50.

Down
1 skull and cross bones
2 island
4 rum
6 pistol
10 crew

Across
3 plank
5 marooned
7 chest
8 treasure
9 bold
10 cutlass

Crossword Puzzle

Clues

Down

1 What is on the pirate flag. (4 words)
2 The treasure is buried on it.
4 Grog.
6 A type of gun used by the pirates.
10 All the people on the ship.

Across

3 Hangs out over the edge of the ship.
5 Punishment for a pirate. Being left behind.
7 The treasure is buried in it.
8 'X' marks the spot where you'll find it.
9 Pirates are always like this.
10 A type of sword used by a pirate.

Can you break the code?
Here's an easy one to
begin.
Each letter is written as a number.

A is 1, B is 2 and so on. Z is 26.

8, 1, 22, 5   2, 21, 18, 9, 5, 4   20, 18, 5, 1, 19, 21, 18, 5   9, 14

— — — —   — — — — — —   — — — — — — — —   — —

3, 1, 22, 5   1, 20   14, 15, 18, 20, 8   5, 14, 4   15, 6

— — — —   — —   — — — — —   — — —   — —

20, 8, 5   9, 19, 12, 1, 14, 4

— — —   — — — — — —

Now try this one.

A B C	D E F	G H I
J K L	M N O	P Q R
S T U	V W	X Y Z

It works like this

A = ⠁
B = ⠃
D = ⠙
R = ⠗

— — — —   — — — —   — —   — — — — — —   — — — —

Reproducible pages

Here is a 'Pirate Game' for you to finish making. Look at the pictures and write in what is happening.
Use dice and counters and play your game.

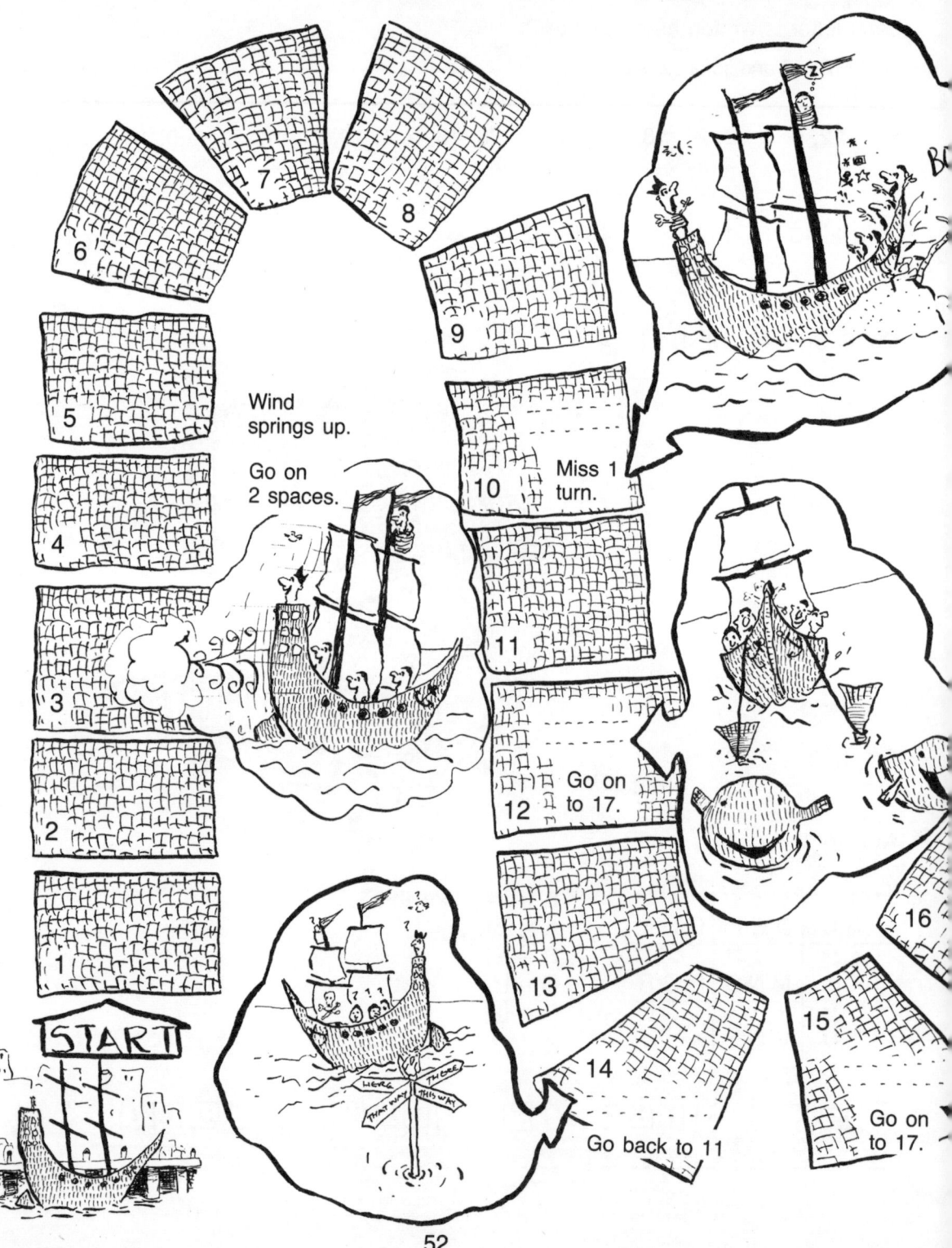

Wind springs up.

Go on 2 spaces.

Miss 1 turn.

Go on to 17.

Go back to 11

Go on to 17.

START

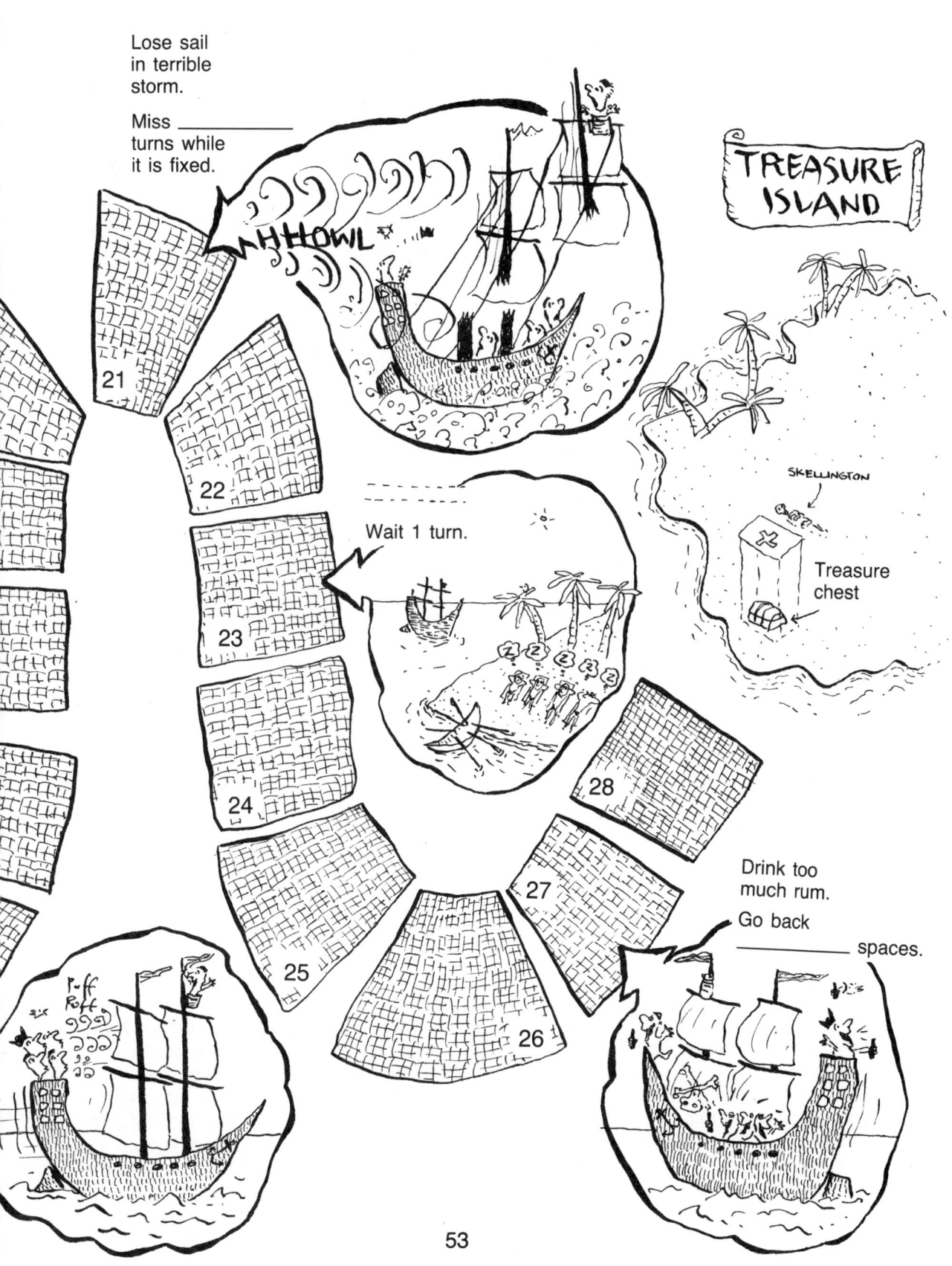

Lose sail in terrible storm.

Miss _____ turns while it is fixed.

TREASURE ISLAND

SKELLINGTON

Treasure chest

21

22

Wait 1 turn.

23

24

25

26

27

28

Drink too much rum.

Go back _____ spaces.

53

THEME
Cats

Session 1

Introduce the theme by allowing children time to browse through a display of picture story and fiction books about cats.

Activities

Children compile a list of cat characters from past reading or the book display. Write two or three sentences about one of these characters using the following format:
  The character's name
  Where the story took place
  The adventure it had

Draw a picture to illustrate your writing, using the sentences. The pictures may be compiled into a booklet and introduced to other grades as 'Our favourite cat stories'.

Session 2

Read *The church mouse* by Oakley.

Discuss

How was Samson different from other cats?
Recall the ways in which Samson was able to help the mice catch the thief.
What do you think was the most exciting part of the story?
Where does the story take place?

Activity

Make an origami cat, using the instructions on page 57. Some children could paint a mural of the church. Construct a display with the mural, origami cats and cut out mice.

Session 3

Read 'Cat' by Eleanor Farjeon in *Oxford book of poetry for children*; 'The cat' by Mary Miller in *5's, 6's and 7's*.

Discuss

In what ways do the two poems differ?
List words that each poet has used to describe cats.
How are these cats different from the one in Session 2?

Activities

Have the children recite the poems. This may be done as a group recital or with individual children saying specific lines.
Distribute copies of the poems to the children to encourage future reading and perhaps memorizing of the poetry.
There is a large selection of poems about cats from which to choose, so make poetry cards for the class, that is, copy the poems on to card, have students illustrate them and file them in a poetry cards box.

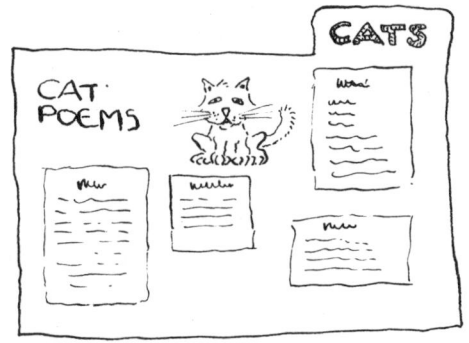

On cat shapes, children write favourite verses selected from poetry collections; display these.

Children could also record names of poems/cat characters/stories on shapes. Include these in a display of origami cats, book jackets, children's writings about cats and photographs of cats to promote further individual reading.

Session 4

Activity

Arrange a cat show, either using children's pet cats or photographs. Invite the local vet to visit and talk about caring for pets, and cats in particular. Declare a 'Be kind to cats week'.

Read from the bibliography more stories and poems about cats.

Session 5

Read *King of the cats* by Galdone.

Discuss

How did you feel as you listened to the story?
What is the mood of the story?
How does the illustrator help to create this mood?
(Look at the faces of the people and the background colour of the pictures.)
Who became king of the cats?
Were you surprised?

Activity

Retell the story inviting the children to participate with 'miaow', and the lines with surprise endings.

'Tell Tom Tildrum that Tim Toldrum's dead'.
Say other tongue-twisters based on the names of people, for example, 'Peter Piper'; make up your own tongue-twisters.

Children compile a list of superstitions about black cats.

Make a cartoon illustration for one of these.

Session 6

Read in serial form, *Carbonel* by Sleigh. If interest is high, develop an ongoing unit of work for *Carbonel* similar to those for *The golden bird* and *Greensmoke* on pages 62 and 66.

Bibliography

Cameron, P. *The cat who thought he was a tiger* (Putnam)

Gag, Wanda *Millions of cats* (Faber/Puffin)

Galdone, Paul *King of the cats* (World's Work)

Leman, M. *Ten cats and their tales* (Pelham)

Oakley, Graham *The church mouse* (Macmillan)

Peppe, Rodney *The cat and the mouse* (Puffin)

Sleigh, Barbara *Carbonel* (Puffin)

Smyth, Gwenda *A pet for Mrs Arbuckle* (Hamilton)

Sutton, Eve *My cat likes to hide in boxes* (Puffin)

Wagner, J. *John Brown, Rose and the midnight cat* (Puffin)

1 Fold a square piece of paper along line
BD (Fig. 1) so that corner C falls on corner A
(Fig. 2).

2 Fold along EF (Fig. 2), bringing corners C
and A forward (Fig. 3). EF is about one-third
of the way down CO (Fig. 2).

3 Fold along OM (Fig. 3), bringing corner D
up so that OD meets F (Fig. 4).

4 Repeat step 3 on the other side at ON
(Figs. 4 & 5).

5 Turn the paper over and draw the face.

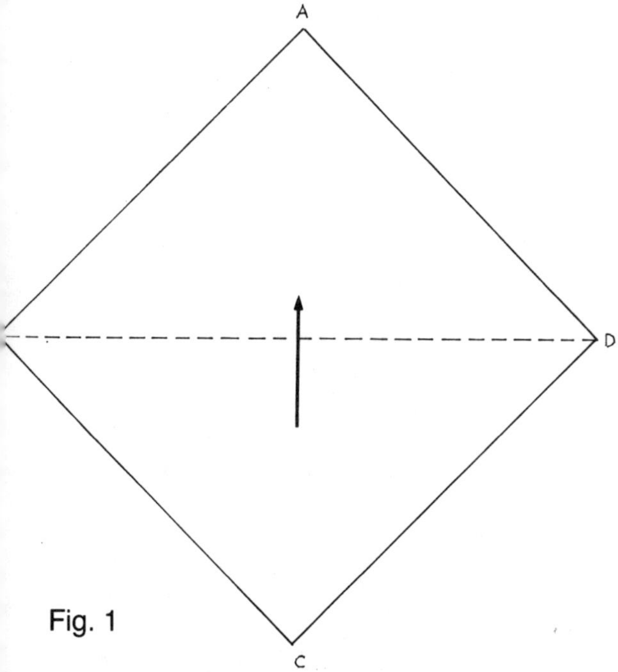

Fig. 1

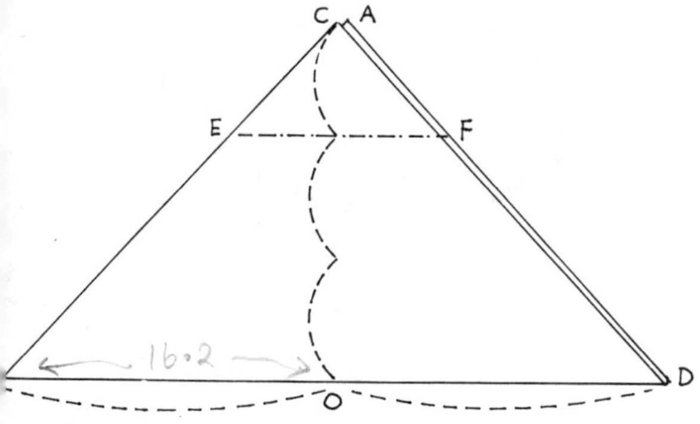

Fig. 2

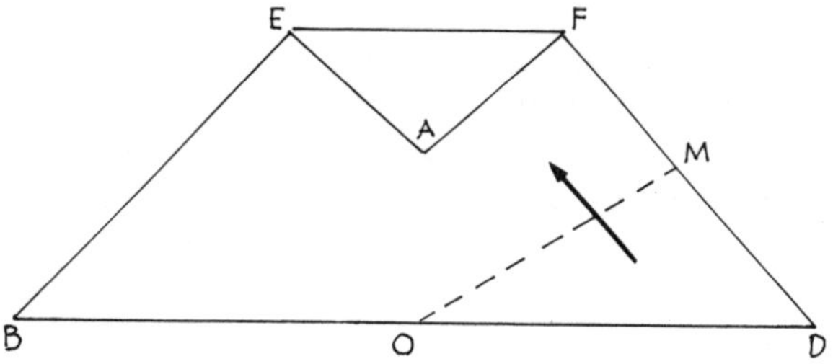

Fig. 3

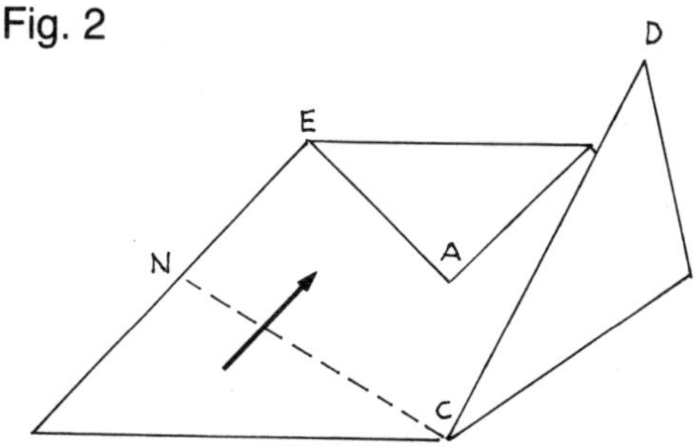

Fig. 4

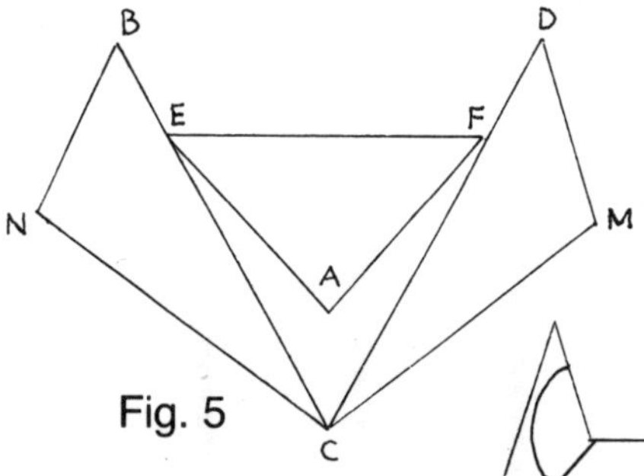

Fig. 5

THEME
Dogs

Introduce the dog theme by reading the series of books by Frank Muir about 'What-a-mess'. Using books from the bibliography, develop a unit similar to 'Harry the dirty dog' on page 21 in Level 1.

Throughout the study provide a regular input of literature from the books suggested in the bibliography.

Dogs as pets

Conduct a survey of the people in your class to find how many have pets. Record the types of pets and show the results on a graph. You may like to broaden the survey to include other classes or even the whole school. Graph your results in one of the following ways.

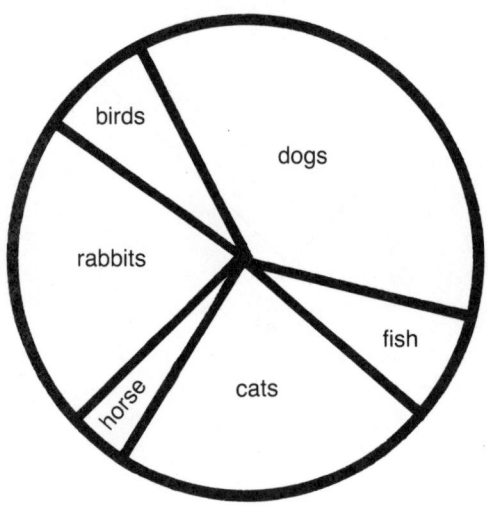

Pie graph

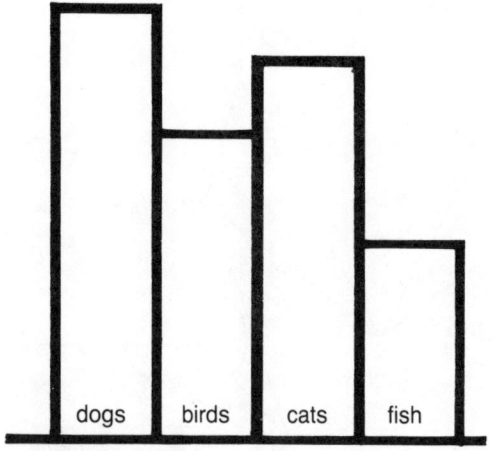

Bar graph

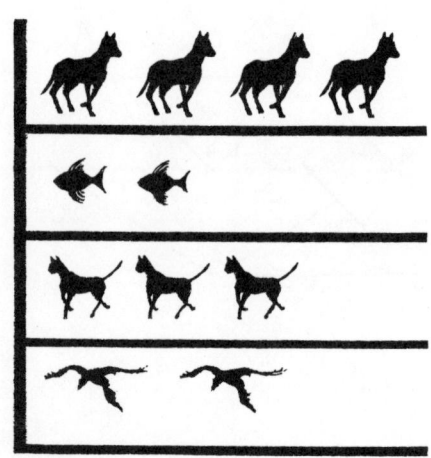

Pictograph

58

Survey the dog owners to determine the most popular dogs.

Discuss

What do you feed a dog?
Where does it sleep?
How do you keep it clean?
What equipment do you need to own if you have a pet dog?
What are some of the problems of keeping a dog?
What exercise does a dog need?
Should dogs be kept in the house?
Why shouldn't big dogs be kept in small yards?
Why do dogs bury bones?
From what diseases do dogs suffer?
How does the shape, length of hair, size of ears etc. affect dogs, e.g. Spaniels (ear problems), Dachsunds (back trouble)?
How do dogs 'talk' to us?

These questions may be discussed in oral sessions and/or be the questions for individual or group assignment work. The answers to the questions may be 'looked up' in reference books or be the basis for a questionnaire to local pet shop owners, veterinary doctors or neighbours who own dogs. Encourage the children to conduct a survey of these local experts as an alternative to book resources.

Bibliography

Balderson, M. *A dog called George* (Oxford University Press)
Berg, L. *My dog Sunday* (Puffin)
Bridwell, N. *Clifford's good deeds* (Scholastic)
Burningham, J. *Cannonball Simp* (Cape)
Cleary, B. *Henry and Ribsy* (Collins Lions)
DeFossard, E. *Dinah the dog with a difference* (one of series in English, Croatian, Greek, Turkish, Italian) (Childerset)
Muir, F. *What a mess* (Benn)
Stern, M. *It's a dog's life* (Cape)

Poems about dogs

Richards, Laura E. 'Jippy and Jimmy' in *Time for poetry* (Scott Forseman)
Chute, Marchett 'Dogs' in *Poems children will sit still for* (Citation Press)

PICTURE STORY BOOKS

Single picture-book activities

Read *When the wind changed* by Park.

Discuss

Talk about this and other superstitions known by the children.

Activities

Using a polaroid camera, take a before-and-after 'the wind changed' photo of each child. Compile these photos into a class album.

Write or tell a personal story explaining how a particular predicament occurred and how the change was affected.

Read *Knees* by MacLeod.

Activity

Expose your knees; everyone exposes their knees and invites a friend to use body paint to decorate the knees.
Have a 'Knees show' and parade.
Involve the whole school community.

No-text picture-books provide an opportunity for children to create their own stories using information obtained from the illustration.

Teachers should therefore be careful not to impose their ideas of a story's development on children.

Show *Sunshine* by Ormerod.
As each page of the book is displayed encourage children to provide a commentary.

Discuss

How does the morning routine in this book compare with that in your house?
Who gets up first in your house?
Who runs late? Who makes breakfast?

Activity

Make up a menu for your favourite breakfast.
Outline either in pictures or words your morning routine.
Read other no-text picture-books, for example, *Anno's journey* by Anno; *Vicki* by Mayer; *The snowman* by Briggs; *Up and up* by Hughes; *One hunter* by Hutchins; *River* by Keeping.

Discuss

Before the story, discuss why some people do not like pets in the house.
What pets are kept by the children?
What do their pets enjoy doing?

Read *Thing* by Robin Klein.

Discuss

Thing's behaviour is like/unlike ordinary pets.
Why is Mrs McIlvray so grumpy?
What would have happened if Thing hadn't stopped growing?
What would have happened if Thing hadn't helped catch the robbers?
What would you have done, if you were Emily, to keep Thing out of the museum?

Activities

Make a collection of pet rocks.
Make a pictograph of pets kept by the class. What's the most popular pet?
Make a chart about Thing which lists:

Food   **Hobbies**   **Favourite TV programs**

Play the 'freeze game'. Turn yourself into different shapes like Thing does.

Read *Dragon's breath* by Dugan.

Discuss

Why are people often afraid of things before they understand or know about them? Has this happened to you?
Why were the people afraid of the dragon?
Why didn't they make friends like Adina did?
Do you like the illustrations? Why did the illustrator use black and white? How do they make you feel?

Activity

Using charcoal or black chalk, draw some illustrations of your own of a gloomy forest, a dragon, or a scene of a bush fire. Display the pictures.

Study of picture-books by one author/illustrator.

See the approach to this study in Level 1 page 18. Authors appropriate to this level are Bill Peet, Mercer Meyer, Stephen Kellog, Tomi De Paola, Victor Ambrus, and Charlotte Zolotow.
Australian authors/illustrators for study at this level are Ron Brooks, Ted Greenwood, Judith Crabtree, and Rhonda and David Armitage.

BOOK STUDIES – FICTION

Introduction

The books listed below are suitable for serial reading to children at this level. While it is not the authors' intention that all of the following activities be undertaken for each book, the studies do provide opportunities for children to interact with literature through writing, drawing, and discussion.

It is the teacher's role to choose those activities which are best suited to the children's interests and ability. In the course of serial reading, it may only be appropriate to introduce activities for one or two chapters.

Finally, the approach taken with these studies may be applied to other novels. *The golden bird* by Edith Brill; *Greensmoke* by Rosemary Manning; *The Iron Man* by Ted Hughes.

The golden bird
by Edith Brill

Chapter 1

Discuss

When do you think the story happened: past, present, or future?
What clues are given to help you decide the time and setting?

If you had been given three wishes, what would you have wished for?
What do we know about the Queen so far?
What do you think of Babka?

Activity

Draw or paint Babka using the description given in Chapter 1.

Chapter 2

Activities

Make a map of the forest. Include Babka's house, the place where the chestnuts grow, the village at the forest edge, Babka's garden, the stream. Reread parts of Chapter 1 for a description of the garden.
Make a list of the characters met so far. This list will be added to as the story progresses.
Make a timetable or chart of Babka's daily activities.

Discuss

Talk about freedom/captivity.
The nut maiden had left her shoes behind when she first met the Prince. What other story do you know where shoes were left behind?
Have the class retell the story of 'Cinderella'.

Activity

Taste chestnuts (if available).

Chapter 3

Activity

Design a maze leading to Wanda's house in the great park.
Include the details described at the beginning of Chapter 3 (rose bushes, bridge, pool, deer, etc.).

Discuss

What has happened to the nut maiden? Predict events. Will she come back? Record predictions and compare with the story later.

Activity

Draw four pictures of Babka's part of the forest to show each season, and how the seasons change.

Chapter 4

Vocabulary

List descriptive words for each of the main characters listed after Chapter 2. Add the dwarf to the list and describe him.
Mime his walk and compare it to Wanda's walk and way of moving.

Activity

Draw the dwarf,
or
make a papier maché mask for the dwarf.

Related stories

What other stories do you know about dwarfs?
Look for stories about dwarfs in the 398 section of the library.
Read or tell some of these.
Write a story about a dwarf.

Chapter 5

Vocabulary

Explain the word 'dowry'.
What was/is this custom?
Add Joseph and Bat Ears to the characters list.

Discuss

Discuss the style of illustration used in the book.
Look at other Pienkowski illustrations.

Other books

Necklace of raindrops and *Kingdom under the sea*, both written by Joan Aiken.

Activity

Draw or paint a scene with 'Bat Ears'.

Chapter 6

Activities

Taste some sunflower seeds.
Plant some as a science experiment; they should be growing by the time you finish the story.

Discuss

Describe the magician. Make up spells and chants. What things are 'golden'?

Related story

Read and then act out the story of 'King Midas and the golden touch'.

Vocabulary

Find out about base metals, crucible.

Chapter 7

Activity

Act out the trial as each witness gives evidence before the judge.

Chapter 8

Activity

Draw a plan of the palace grounds.

Discuss

What do we know of the history of witches, witch trials and burnings/dunking?
Share other stories about witches.

Library

A group of children may like to research information about witches and report back to the class.

Collect all the books you can about witches from the library for a classroom reading corner.

Vocabulary

Up-date the characters list.
Up-date the descriptive words for each character.

Discuss

What does the 'Grey Gander' mean? Make predictions as to its influence on the story.
Who do you like most in the story so far? Why?

Chapters 9 and 10

Activity

Map Babka's journey to find the Grey Gander.

Discuss

Talk about bird migration.

Chapter 11

Activity

Make a model of a snow house.
Does anybody live in snow houses today? How are they built?

Discuss

What dangers are there in the snow? What is hypothermia?
How are stars used to guide travellers?

Story making

Help class create a story to tell about Nonno and Bonno.
Who are they?
What are they?
How did they come to be there?
What do they do?

Chapter 12

Discuss

Talk about starvation.
How much food do we need to survive?
Compare predictions about the Grey
Gander, made after Chapter 8, with the
King's story.

Chapter 13

Discuss

What is kindness?
Talk about good deeds.
Should we expect something in return?
What is bribery?

Chapters 14 and 15

Activities

Make a wall mural of the procession into
the palace.

Display all items produced and invite
other grades to come and look. Each
child is to escort a visitor and explain the
items in the display: the way they were
made; their significance to the story.

Other activities

Retell the main events in sequence, as
illustrations or in writing.

Make this into a filmstrip and tape a
commentary.

Write a book-review letter to tell others
how much you enjoyed the story.

Write a newspaper report for one of the
events in the story, e.g. Babka's trial,
finding the King, the death of the Queen.

Read these on to a tape recorder as a
radio news report.

Design a newspaper headline for one of
the events.
Example:

Write to the author and the illustrator
summing up the feelings of the group.
Address your letters 'care of the
publisher'. Authors and illustrators
generally enjoy hearing from their
audience.

Use vocabulary lists about the characters
to write 'Who am I?' puzzles.

Write 'Where am I?' puzzles for different
settings used in the story.

Greensmoke
by Rosemary Manning

Chapter 1

Discuss

What do you do at the beach?
What might you find?
What games do you play?
Tell about a time you had at the beach.

Activities

Draw a beach scene as described in the chapter.
Pictorially represent the story line for Chapter 1 (see below).
Sing 'Lavender's blue' adapted by the dragon to become 'Dragon's are red . . .' (see page 19).

Vocabulary

Explain 'elevenses'; centuries; humble.

Activity

Depict the story line in a series of labelled illustrations.

Record of the work

Make a booklet for each child by stapling 8–10 pages together. Use a coloured cover paper for the front page. Record bibliographic details: title, author, illustrator.
This booklet may be used for written and art activities for the duration of the study.

Chapter 2

Discuss

Does Susan's mother believe in dragons? How do you think the papers with the songs get to Susan's bedroom?

Talk about tides.
Why is there a low and high point?

Activities

Make a list of the characters introduced so far. This list will be extended as the story progresses.

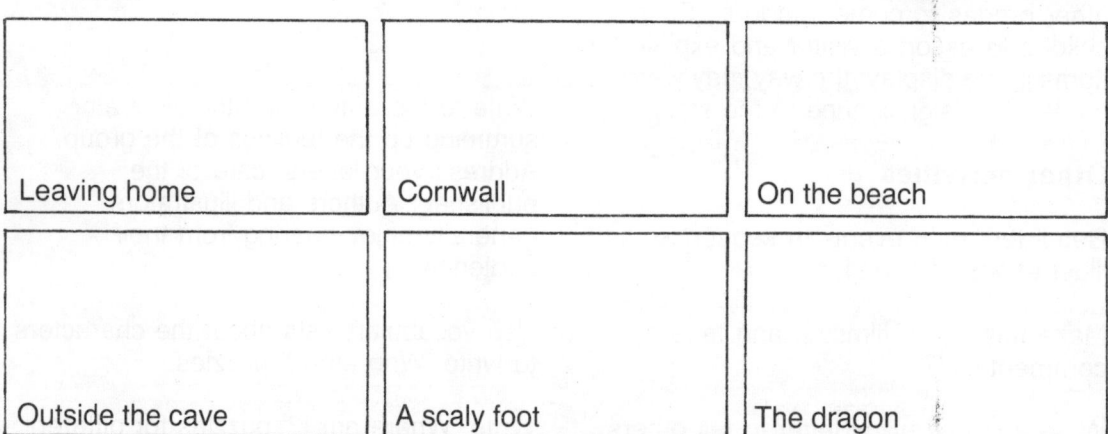

Leaving home	Cornwall	On the beach
Outside the cave	A scaly foot	The dragon

Paint or draw a before-and-after portrait of 'Merlin the magician'.

Illustrate 'The fiery dragon above the enchanted forest'.

Related stories

Lion in the meadow by Margaret Mahy (Penguin); *The dragon of an ordinary family* by Margaret Mahy (Heinemann).

Chapter 3

Discuss

Talk about other saints that you know. Why are they 'famous'?

Library

Find books about saints, King Arthur, dragons.
Borrow these for a classroom reading corner.

Vocabulary

Compile word lists to describe the dragon
● before he was tamed by St. Petroc
● as he now appears in the story.

Include a 'menu' of his meals at both of these times.

Related story

'Stan Bolovan' in *A book of dragons* by Ruth Manning-Sanders (Methuen)

Chapter 4

Discuss

Was the farmer's boy right to take the King of France's goblet? (This discussion could take the form of a debate.)
Where in the world, would you like to go if the fairies gave you the chance? Why?

Research

Using an atlas, locate:
   Cornwall
   France
   Scotland
   Ireland
   Honolulu

Activity

Draw a picture of the view Susan had from the dragon's back.

Chapter 5

Discuss

What would be the most suitable name for the dragon?
Have each child choose a name.
Graph the choice of names to show the most popular.
Wait until the end of the story to see if the name is revealed — it never is.
Hold a ballot to give the dragon a name.

Vocabulary

Add words to the list which describe the dragon now that the author has revealed more of his character (sulky, bad-tempered, impatient).

How many words can you make with the letters of the word 'Excalibur'.

(rib, rub, race, ace, brace, crab, bale, bail, care, bare, Alice, ear, lice, Ali, Rex, etc. There are at least 20).

Related stories

Retell the story of Rumpelstiltskin (Grimm).
Dramatize this story.
Make stick puppets for the characters.
What other stories do you know that were written by the Grimm brothers?
Check the 398 section of the library.

Chapter 6

Activities

Sing 'Oranges and lemons' (Play the game as an activity session); 'I had a little nut tree'.

Add words to up-date list.
Classify them: real/imaginary; good/bad.

Vocabulary

Write cinquain verse about mermaids. (See p.100 for an explanation of 'cinquain'.)

Discuss

What do you know about the lost city of Atlantis?

Related stories

Atlantis; the missing continent by David McMullin (Raintree); *A book of mermaids* by Ruth Manning-Sanders (Methuen).

Chapter 7

Activities

Sing 'Old Macdonald . . .'.
The children retell a familiar giant story, such as 'Jack and the beanstalk'.

Related stories

A book of giants by Ruth Manning-Sanders (Methuen); *A book of giant stories* by David L. Harrison (Jonathan Cape); *Jim and the beanstalk* by Raymond Briggs (Hamish Hamilton) (compare this story to the traditional 'Beanstalk' version).

Activity

Make buns.
1 cup self-raising flour; 1 pinch of salt; 2 tablespoons margarine; 2 tablespoons sugar; 2 tablespoons milk.
Sift flour and salt. Rub in margarine. Add sugar. Stir in milk.
Mixture shouldn't be too sticky.
Knead dough till smooth, then cut it into 9 pieces. Roll these pieces into ball shapes and place on a baking tray.
Poke a hole in the top of each bun and fill with jam.
Paint each bun with milk.
Bake for 10–12 minutes at 450°F/230°C.

Chapter 8

Discuss

What are star constellations?
Refer to the library non-fiction collection at 523.

Chapter 9

Discuss

Find the origin of personal names. The introduction to the *World book dictionary* has a useful list of these. Other useful books are *The story of surnames* by Lilian Devereus (Blackwell); *What's in a name*? by Leslie Alan Dunkling (Rigby).

Chapter 10

Research

Use library resources to find information about other mythical creatures: unicorns; bunyips; centaur; griffin; Minotaur; Cyclops.

Make a grade book of 'Mythical beasts'.

Read Greek, Roman, Celtic mythology. Many of the stories have been adapted for younger readers. Investigate the 398 section of the library.

Find information on the life of a knight. Group topics could include:
    Food they ate and how it was obtained
    Life inside the castle
    The clothes they wore: armour, chain mail
    Entertainments: music, storytelling, jousts, tournaments
    Weapons for a 'knight'.

Subject headings used in the library catalogue for information about this topic are:
    Knights and knighthood
    Chivalry
    Arthur, King
    Heraldry
    Middle Ages
    Castles

Activities

Write a story about 'The day Susan called up the dragon'.
Tell about
    the main characters
    the places Susan visited
    the funniest or most exciting incident
    your favourite story told by the dragon
    the song you liked the best.
Display the reviews for all to see.
Make a 'bottle top knight' or an 'egg carton dragon' (see *Model from junk* by Brenda B. Jackson (Evans)).
Cut out cardboard characters as mobile hangings.

The Iron Man
by Ted Hughes

Chapter 1

Discuss

Where do you think the Iron Man came from?
What happened to his second ear?
Each part of the Iron Man was independent. What was the most important part?
What is the most important part of your body?

Chapter 2

Discuss

Does the Iron Man seem real?
What makes him work?
Why did Hogarth trap the Iron Man?
What other trapping methods might he have used?
Who do you know that uses traps?
Why don't the farmers like the Iron Man?
How would you have felt if you were confronted by this 'monster'?
Why should Hogarth feel guilty?

Chapter 3

Discuss

What has been happening to the Iron Man while he was buried underground?
What was it that aroused him?
How did Hogarth solve the problem of what to do with the Iron Man?
What might have happened if Hogarth hadn't solved the problem?

Chapter 4

Discuss

Why did the Iron Man take so long to speak for the first time?
How will the Iron Man champion the world?
What is panic?
What things make an individual, or a group, panic?

Chapter 5

Discuss

How is the Iron Man changed during the story?
How have the people changed?
What might have happened if the Iron Man had not won the contest with the Space Bat Angel Dragon?

Vocabulary

From chapter one onwards, prepare vocabulary charts for each of the main characters.
List words used by the author to describe the characters after the reading of each chapter. Add words suggested by the children.
These lists will be a resource for writing activities.

Characterization

Write brief character sketches using words from the vocabulary lists.
Do this at different stages in the story and compare the changes in characters as the story progresses.

Activities

Map and label the setting of each chapter.
Chart the Iron Man's progress through the countryside.

Investigate the rhythm of machinery.
With the use of the rhythm, work as a machine using arms only.
Work as a machine using arms and legs.
With a partner, work as a machine with arms only.
Groups of four or five work as a machine using all parts of the body.
Provide an outline of an incident from the story and allow groups to prepare a dramatization.

On a table top construct the village, the countryside, cliff top and other settings used in the story.
Use cut out characters to 'people' the settings.

Draw the view of the Iron Man as seen by the seagulls.

Design a poster to advertise the book to others.

Construct headline posters for the Iron Man's adventures and for the arrival of the Space Bat Angel Dragon, and for the duel between the Iron Man and the Space Bat Angel Dragon.

Write newspaper, TV, and radio news reports on a continuing basis throughout the story.
Approach the newspaper reports from the various standpoints of:
    a women's magazine
    a daily newspaper
    a sporting paper.

Make a menu. Compile a day's eating for Iron Man.

Breakfast: _____

Lunch: _____

Dinner: _____

What might the eating places be called?
For example: 'The Old Tip Restaurant'.
Invent recipes for an Iron Man diet.
For example: Nuts and bolts pie.
              Terrine of oiled sump.

Use a comic strip format to retell each chapter.
Try to do it with and without captions.
Make a picture story book version of the story. Use two or three illustrations for each chapter.

Make an Iron Man dice game which sequences the events of the story.

Write a letter to a friend telling what it is like to be in Australia now that the Space Bat Angel Dragon has landed.
Other stories by Ted Hughes are *How the whale became and other stories; Nessie the mannerless monster; Meet my folks* (a collection of poetry).

Level 3 Ages 10–12

Framework for Ages 10–12 literature program

Activities

Themes
   Colour
   Heroes
   Dogs
Picture story books
   Picture story books for older
   children
   Single picture-book activities
A poetry starter
Book talks
Book discussion groups
Book studies — Fiction:
   Mrs. Frisby and the rats of Nimh by
   Robert O'Brien
   Dragon slayer by Rosemary Sutcliff
   The turbulent term of Tyke Tiler by
   Gene Kemp
   The midnight fox by Betsy Byars
   The boy who was afraid by Armstrong
   Sperry

Framework for Age 10 literature program

Abilities to be reached	Teaching points	Literary forms appropriate for level
Distinguish between realism and fantasy in fiction books and explain the difference.	Could the story really have happened? Are people like this? Relate actions of characters in fantasy stories to real life.	Picture story Poetry Story-telling
Identify themes in novels and relate to real life.	How would you have behaved in the situations described in these novels? What do you think the author is trying to make us think about?	Short story collections Fiction (Fantasy, humour, realism, science fiction).
Describe the storyline development in particular novels: setting, problem, climax, ending.	Use the following format to construct the storyline development of particular books.	Myths and legends Drama

Setting	Problem	Climax	Ending
Beginning (Who, when, where).	Action starts	Biggest problem	Problem is solved.

Abilities to be reached	Teaching points	Literary forms appropriate for level
Describe personality changes that occur in characters.	From what you have read, do you know more about the character at the end of the story, than you did at the beginning? What events contributed to the change in personality? Did you expect these changes?	
Identify locale, and setting.	Children make maps of journeys undertaken in stories. Draw plans of locations. Illustrate same location at different times and in different seasons.	
Identify premeditated or spontaneous actions carried out by characters in particular novels.	In your opinion, was the main character's behaviour right or wrong? Why did the character behave the way he or she did?	

Framework for Ages 11 and 12 literature program

Abilities to be reached	Teaching points	Literary forms appropriate for level
Distinguish between historical and contemporary fiction and biographical books, and explain differences.	Read selections from each type and discuss differences. Compile a definition for each of these types.	Picture story Poetry Story-telling
Identify the theme in a particular novel and evaluate extent to which it is realistic as opposed to being over-simplified or didactic.	Compare books on a similar theme and discuss the variation of treatment. Use a group-reading approach to examine several books on the same theme, e.g. war, fear.	Short story collections Fiction (Fantasy, humour, realism, historical, biographical, science fiction).
Describe the storyline development in particular novels: setting, problem, climax, ending.	Continue activity outlined in framework for age 10. Children also write stories using storyline framework.	Epics Drama
Evaluate the believability of characters from novels read.	What part of the story best describes the main character? Can the characters be related to real life? Does the author give enough information about the character for us to believe in him or her? Do you know anyone like this? Write a character profile of a friend.	
Identify locale, time and social aspects of setting.	Discuss, using extracts from novels, comparisons of accepted behaviours, social mores. Read descriptive passages illustrating an aspect of setting; children draw or discuss their impressions.	
Relate emotions identified in fiction books to own emotional experiences and needs.	How did the author make you feel this way? Display extracts which highlight a particular emotion.	

THEME
Colour

Session 1

Discuss

How is colour used in our environment?
Red for danger, attracts attention.
Yellow is for safety.
Blue is used to indicate coolness.
What things could never be blue?
Traditional uses for colour:
   black — mourning
   white — weddings.
Classify colours and moods.
Read *Oh! Were they ever happy* by
Spier.

Activity

Make a colour wheel.
Colour both circles as shown on either
side of heavy cardboard.

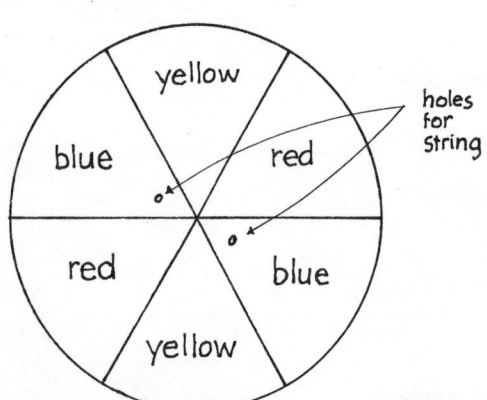

Put two strings through the two holes
near the centre.
Spin the disc until string is twisted tight.
Pull on the string, then draw it in until the
disc spins faster and faster. What
happens?

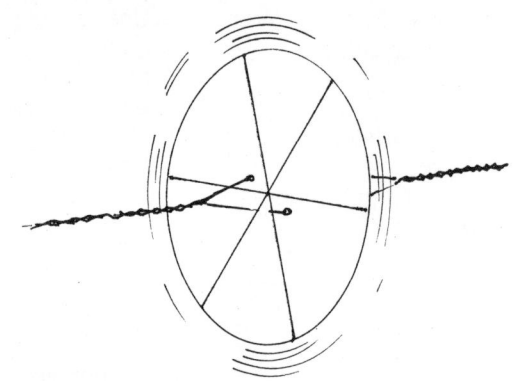

Session 2

Read Selections from *Hailstones and
halibut bones* by O'Neill.

Discuss

What are the various moods that the
author has associated with each colour?

Activity

Write verses about colour. This may be
done either as group or individual work.
Provide a model for the children's writing
by analysing the approach used by Mary
O'Neill.

Session 3

Discuss

Common expressions which refer to colour are
   as red as a beetroot
   a green thumb
   in the pink
   feeling blue
   like a red rag to a bull
   black as the ace of spades
   every cloud has a silver lining
   seeing the world through
   rose-coloured glasses.

Activities

Make illustrations for each of the expressions above and compile them into a book.

Attempt to explain the origins of the expressions in an original short story.
Read extracts from *Blue Fin* by Colin Thiele which highlight colours associated with the sea.

Session 4

Read 'Jason and the quest for the golden fleece' by Roger Lancelyn Green.

Discuss

How believable are the story and its characters? Why have stories about heroes and magical beasts been part of our heritage?

Activity

Make a map of the journey taken by Jason and his Argonauts.

Session 5

Activity

Use questions for literature games 'Which colour?' listed on page 122, for a quiz contest.

Read *The great blueness and other predicaments* by Arnold Lobel. For activities based on this book see page 8.

Retelling

Sequence the events of *The great blueness* . . . or of 'Jason and the quest for the golden fleece' in six or eight illustrations. Use these as the focus for an oral retelling session.

Session 6

Activities

Conduct a survey of family and friends to determine the most favoured colour. Graph the results.

Write a televison commercial to sell yellow, or any other colour.

Read *Jumanji* by Allsburg, which uses black and white illustrations. Contrast this with the use of full colour in *The sea people* by Muller and Steiner.

Discuss

What effects can be produced with the use of colour?

Session 7

Activities

Screen the 16 mm film *The red balloon*. Look at the picture-book version of the story which uses stills from the movie.

Sing 'Follow the yellow brick road' from the *Wizard of Oz*. (Introduce the book at the same time).

Session 8

Activity

Have a 'colour day'. This can be an event for the whole school or just your class.
Have a green day, or red day if you'd prefer.

Everyone comes dressed in the colour chosen.
Make coloured drinks and coloured food for lunch.
Refer to Theme — Colour in Level 1 for ideas and titles which may be appropriate at this level.

Bibliography

Allsburg, Chris Van *Jumanji* (Houghton Mifflin)

Green, Roger 'Jason and the quest for the golden fleece' in *Tales of Greek Heroes* (Puffin)

Lamorisse, Albert *The red balloon* (Allen & Unwin)

Lobel, Arnold *The great blueness . . .* (Collins)

Muller, J. & Steiner, J. *The sea people* (Victor Gollancz)

O'Neill, Mary *Hailstones and halibut bones* (World's Work)

Spier, Peter *Oh! Were they ever happy* (Doubleday)

Thiele, Colin *Blue Fin* (Rigby)
See also bibliography for colour theme, Level 1.

THEME
Heroes

An assignment approach

Using one of the legendary heroes below, for example, Beowulf, and focusing on characterization, the teacher explores with the children the literature that has been written about this individual.

David and	Theseus	Samson
Goliath	Icarus	Jason
Ulysses	Sinbad	Robin Hood
Beowulf	Perseus	King Arthur
Joan of Arc	Pegasus	
William Tell		

Start by reading page 29 of *Dragon slayer* by Sutcliff (Penguin edition).

Discuss

What aspects of character are revealed in the extract?
Children could illustrate their interpretations.
Explain the following, using maps/diagrams:
   Beowulf's place in time/location setting
   why the character is a hero (Read p. 65 of *Dragon slayer* to highlight this.)

Activity

Display a poster advertising the hero:

THE AGE
Beowulf downs Sea Hag

Read or tell the rest of the legend in serial form; children proceed with group activity, as outlined in next section.
(A detailed study of *Dragon slayer*, the story of Beowulf by Rosemary Sutcliff, can be found on p.101.)

Beowulf the Goth

Grendel came to Heorot,
  The kingliest of halls,
And took his supper on the spot
  Within those golden walls:
On many a Dane he made again
  His meal with lips a-froth —
'But you shall not sup on me, Grendel!'
  Said Beowulf the Goth.

Grendel howled in Heorot
  Between the walls of gold,
For the strongest man alive had got
  The monster in his hold.
He caught him tight, as others might
  Have caught a little moth —
'And now your hour is come, Grendel!'
  Said Beowulf the Goth.

Grendel fled from Heorot
  With golden splinters strewn,
But the fair hall stood without a blot
  Before the next night's moon.
Now clear and strong rose sounds of song
  Instead of sounds of wrath —
'For you have supped your last, Grendel!'
  Said Beowulf the Goth.

Eleanor Farjeon from *The Childrens' Bells* (OUP)

Group activity

Following the introduction of Beowulf, and if interest warrants, teacher sets up a framework in which groups of children explore the literature about a chosen legendary hero.
1 Form groups on basis of interest in particular hero.
2 Children decide, on looking at the hero, whether their focus will be on plot, theme, style, mood, setting, characterization or a combination of these.
3 Teacher provides an appropriate proforma which sets out suggested tasks to be completed by group (example of a character proforma below).
4 Members of group allocate tasks among themselves.
5 The proforma is completed in searching, reading, talking sessions.
6 If appropriate, organize
  a group presentations
  b displays
  c class discussion comparing legendary heroes with modern counterparts.

Characterization proforma:
This proforma highlights aspects of characterization.

Group members [   ]

Hero [   ]

Tasks
1 Brief explanation of the hero's place in time:
   When did he live?
   Where did he live? (Perhaps find a map and trace journeys.)
2 Discuss the relationship of this hero with other legendary heroes.
3 Explore why the character was a hero — provide a brief character sketch. What was his status in the community (king, soldier, tribal chief, etc.)?
4 Tell or read extracts from a story about the hero.

Individual activities

Make a poster advertising the hero.

Draw a mural or map of the hero's journeys.

Construct a diorama depicting an episode in the hero's life.

Record an 'interview' with the hero.

Dramatize an episode of one of the hero's adventures.

An alternative approach

Tell or read a series of stories about Ulysses: Helen of Troy; the Trojan war and seige; Ulysses and the Wooden Horse; selected adventures of Ulysses as he journeys home; his encounters with Circe and the Cyclops.

As each story is presented some or all of the following activities might be undertaken:
Begin a large wall frieze and add to it as each story is completed.

Make a map tracing the journey to the war and returning home.

Make a model of the wooden horse; the city of Troy; the island of the Cyclops; sailing past the Sirens.

Construct a board game which outlines the journey and sequence of events.

Have class dress up for one of the stories and take photographs. Record the story on tape to accompany slides. Any one of the stories could involve a cast of thousands!

Bibliography

Crossley-Holland, Kevin (illust., Keeping, Charles) *Beowulf* (Oxford University Press)

Fagg, C. *Fabulous beasts* (Ward Lock)

Green, R. *The adventures of Robin Hood* (Puffin)

—— *King Arthur* (Puffin)

—— *Myths of the Norse men* (Puffin)

—— *Tales of Greek heroes* (Puffin)

—— *The tale of Troy* (Puffin)

Manning-Sanders, R. *A book of heroes and heroines* (Methuen)

Mayne, W. *A book of heroes* (Hamish Hamilton)

Preshous, J. D. M. *Famous legends book 1* (Ladybird) *Famous legends book 2* (Ladybird)

Ridsdale, A. *Larger than life* (Nelson Young Australia series)

Samuda, M. *Stories of courage* (Ward Lock)

—— *Heroes and heroines* (Arnold)

Serraillier, I. *Heracles the strong* (Heinemann)

Sutcliff, R. *Dragon slayer; the story of Beowulf* (Puffin)

Treece, H. *Vinland the good* (Puffin) Other historical fiction by this author

Robert Nye - Bee-hunter.

THEME
Dogs

Introduce the theme by reading Henry Lawson's 'The Loaded Dog'. Throughout the development of the theme, provide further literature input by reading selections from the bibliography at the end of this section.

Read one of the novels as a serial, introduce and encourage individual and group reading of the other novels.

Read 'Lone dog' by Irene Rutherford McLeod in *Time for poetry* (Scott Forseman); 'The country dog' by Max Fatchen in *Songs for my dog and other people* (Kestrel).

Dog breeds

List the breeds of dogs known by the children and classify them as
   hunting dogs
   working dogs
   sporting dogs.
Use other classifications suggested by the children.

Working dogs

Which tasks do dogs perform?
Which breeds are most commonly used? Why?
Tasks performed will include:
   guiding
   guarding
   herding
   sled pulling
   hunting
   racing
   entertaining
   detecting

How are dogs trained for the work they do? Contact the police dog squad or the Blind Institute and request a speaker. A local dog-obedience school might also help with a speaker.

Discuss

Dogs are often used by scientists for experiments which test drugs, chemicals, and operations to see if they are safe for humans.
Should this be done?
Read Aesop's fable, 'The dog in the manger'. Discuss the origin of this expression.
Do the students know any other 'dog' sayings?
Introduce
   in the dog house
   dog in the manger
   barking up the wrong tree
   let sleeping dogs lie
   raining cats and dogs
   his bark is worse than his bite
   you can't teach an old dog new tricks
   puppy love
   hang-dog expression.
Make a booklet of 'doggy' sayings.
Write an explanation for the expression and illustrate.

Interesting questions

Find the answers by reading books found in the library or by interviewing people with some knowledge of dogs.

Where does the dog sit on the tucker box?
What is the largest dog in the world?
Which dog doesn't bark?
Which dogs have their tails lopped? Why?
Which is the most popular dog in Australia?
What are some famous dogs? e.g. film stars, Rin-Tin-Tin, Lassie; cartoon dogs, Snoopy, Pluto.
How many different breeds of dog are there?
Which is the fastest dog in the world?
A dog was used in a space experiment — find out about it.

History of the dog

Find out from which animal the dog has descended.
Which ancient peoples kept dogs?
For what purpose were they kept?
The names of dogs often had something to do with their occupation, e.g. bulldogs were used by the British to fight bulls.
Can you find any others?

Find out about famous dogs

Argos
Cerberus
Laika

Mapping

List the names of wild dog breeds:
dingoes
coyotes
wolves
jackals
foxes
On a map of the world show where they live.
Groups of students may like to find out about each of the breeds and prepare a brief report to be displayed.

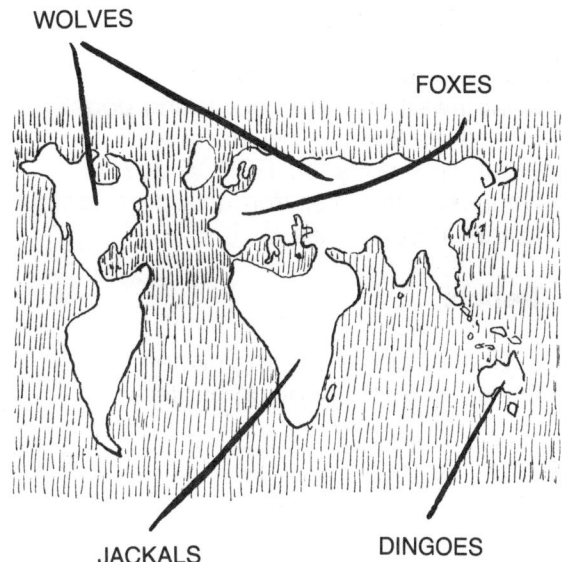

Questions that might be asked:
How do these dogs live?
What is the hierarchy of the pack?
How is it established?
What is the habitat?
What are the breeding/mating habits?
Encourage the students to pose their own questions for 'research'.

A dog's instincts

What instincts/habits do domestic dogs carry over from their wild ancestors?
urinating on fences, trees, etc.
sniffing
rolling over when threatened
tails curled between legs
turning around before lying down
gobbling food
Can you explain this behaviour?

Dogs and science

Pavlov, a famous scientist, used dogs in experiments. Find out about these. What other scientists used dogs?

Dogs and the law

Visit your local council office and find out
what laws there are concerning dogs?
How does the dog catcher work?
What work does the RSPCA do?
Request a speaker from this organization
to talk to your class.

Debate

1 Sheep farmer vs. dog owners
2 Use of traps by dingo hunters

Bibliography

Armstrong, W. *Sounder* (Puffin)
Atkinson, E. *Greyfriars Bobby* (Puffin)
Burnford, S. *The incredible journey* (Hodder)
Byars, B. *The midnight fox* (Puffin)
Davison, F. D. *Dusty* (Angus & Robertson)
Estes, E. *Ginger Pye* (Bodley Head)
George, J. C. *Julie of the wolves* (Harper & Row)
Knight, E. *Lassie come home* (Puffin)
London, J. *Call of the wild* (Hamlyn)
Love, I. F. *For the love of Benji* (Bantam)
Pearce, P. *A dog so small* (Puffin)
Smith, D. *101 Dalmations* (Heinemann)

PICTURE STORY BOOKS

Picture story books for older children

Presenting picture story-books

Read a picture story book daily to your children. (This may for a period of time take the place of, or add to, your serial reading of fiction books.)
1 Selection may be based on a weekly theme, e.g. monsters.
2 Seek advice from your school librarian regarding books.
3 Practise reading the story.
4 Construct questions to stimulate discussion. (For examples see p. 88 'Single picture-book activities'.)
5 Read the story.
  a Seat children comfortably where they are able to see the illustrations.
  b Use a clear voice, with voice characterizations if you feel comfortable doing it.
  c Hold the book still and allow plenty of time for children to explore the visual material.
  d Don't interrupt the story; save questions and comments until the end.
6 Allow a quiet reflective time before launching into discussion.
7 Organize activities if appropriate.

Starting points

1 Occasionally show the pictures before reading, and ask children to predict what the story will be about in terms of setting, mood, characters, and plot.
2 Alternately, read the story without showing the pictures; children predict what the illustrations will contain.
3 Use the illustrations as cues for retelling, after the story has been read.

Looking at technique

1 What art techniques/media has the illustrator used — ink/pencil?
2 How do the illustrations make you feel — sad/happy/uneasy?
3 Is this feeling reflected in the story line? How?
4 Are the characters drawn as realistic figures or caricatures?
5 Compare books using black and white illustrations with those using colour — try to decide why the artist has chosen one in preference to the other.

Looking at types

1 Humour
  Read a selection of humorous picture story-books and decide how each artist has made statements about humour:
  a caricatures, e.g. Mordillo, Peet, Niland
  b bright color, e.g. Pavey
  Examine use of rhyme, nonsense names, strange sounding words e.g. Seuss, Viorst, Axelson.
2 Fantasy/reality
  Read *The dancing tigers* by Hoban and

Jumanji by Allsburg, and explore the relationship between fantasy and reality.
  a Look at plot and characters and examine how the illustrations support their development.
  b Are the illustrations unusual in any respect; technique, placement, size, frequency or subject matter?
  c Is the theme unusual?
3 Trilogies
  What themes/relationships link the following Sendak books: *Where the wild things are; In a night kitchen; Outside over there.*

Activities

One or more of these activities may be appropriate as a follow-up to your reading and discussion of particular picture story books.
1 Detailed examination of an artist's work
  a Collect all the books you can find that have been illustrated by your chosen artist — list them.
  b Make a gallery of the artist's characters.
  c Write a letter to the artist; send it to the publisher's address, which can usually be found on the back of the title page.
2 Looking at types
  a Select a particular type — alphabet books, unusual format.
  b Treat as outlined elsewhere in this section.
3 Compare a particular picture story book with a 16 mm film.
4 Write sequels, verse, advertisements.
5 Make murals, posters, board games, silhouettes, dioramas, slide sets/photographic books about particular picture-books.
6 After all of the above, the children should be ready, either individually or in groups, to produce their own picture story books.

Using the children

Encourage older children to share picture story books with younger children.
This may be done by an older child reading to whole grades, small groups, or individual children.
1 The 'presenter' selects an appropriate book for the audience. The 'presenter' and librarian or teacher discuss the selection.
2 Practise reading the story.
3 Presentation — remember the points outlined elsewhere in this section.
4 Child reports back to teacher or librarian for an evaluation of suitability of selection and method of presentation.

Bibliography

Alexander, L. *The king's fountain* (Dutton)

Allsburg, Chris van *Jumanji* (Houghton Mifflin)

Ambrus, V. *Blackbeard the pirate* (Oxford University Press)

Anderson, W. *Ratsmagic* (Ape)

Axelsen, S. *The oath of Bad Brown Bill* (Nelson/Puffin)

Barrett, J. *Cloudy with a chance of meatballs* (Atheneum)

Baumann, K. *Mickey's kitchen contest* (Childerset)

Briggs, R. *Father Christmas* (Hamilton/Puffin)

—— *Fungus the bogeyman* (Hamilton)

—— *Gentleman Jim* (Hamilton)

—— *Jim and the beanstalk* (Puffin)

Brooks, R. *Aranea* (Puffin)

Cooney, B. *Chanticleer and the fox* (Kestrel)

Crabtree, J. *Legs* (Kestrel)

—— *The sparrow's story at the King's command* (Oxford University Press)

De Paola, T. *The clown of God* (Harcourt Brace Jovanovich)

Dugan, M. *Dragon's breath* (Puffin)

Foreman, M. *War and peas* (Hamish Hamilton)

Galdone, J. *The tailypo* (World's Work)

Hoban, R. *The dancing tigers* (Cape)

Keeping, C. *Joseph's yard* (Oxford University Press)

Lasker, J. *He's my brother* (Whitman)

Lobel, A. *The great blueness and other predicaments* (Collins)

Mahy M. *The wind between the stars* (Dent)

Mayer, M. *One monster after another* (Golden Press)

Mordillo, G. *The galleon* (Quist)

—— *Crazy cowboy* (Quist)

Paterson, A. B. *The man from Ironbark* (Collins)

—— *The man from Snowy River* (Collins)

Rockwell, T. *The neon motorcycle* (Watts)

Roughsey, D. *The giant devil dingo* (Collins)

—— *The rainbow serpent* (Collins)

Sendak, M. *Where the wild things are* (Bodley Head/Puffin)

—— *In a night kitchen* (Bodley Head/Puffin)

—— *Outside over there* (Bodley Head)

Steiner, J. *The bear who wanted to stay a bear* (Hutchinson)

—— *Rabbit Island* (Hutchinson)

Turska, K. *The magician of Cracow* (Greenwillow)

Ungerer, T. *The beast of Monsieur Racine* (Bodley Head)

—— *The hat* (Bodley Head)

Viorst, J. *Alexander and the terrible, awful very bad day* (Angus & Robertson)

—— *The tenth good thing about Barney* (Collins)

Wagner, J. *John Brown, Rose and the midnight cat* (Puffin)

Yeoman, J. *The wild washerwomen* (Hamish Hamilton/Puffin)

PICTURE STORY BOOKS

Single picture-book activities

Read *The wild washerwomen* by Yeoman.

Discuss

How do the women change in this story? What prompted their change?
Look carefully at the last picture in the book; list the tasks that the men and women are doing.
Compare the faces of the washerwomen in the first and last picture of the book; what differences do you notice?
What is the theme of this story?

Activity

Make a list of jobs done by the mothers and fathers of the children in your grade. Are there differences between jobs done by males and females. Do you feel these differences should/should not exist.

Read *Bored — Nothing to do* by Spier.

Discuss

Do you ever get bored? How do you overcome boredom?
How would your parents react if you dismantled everything in the house to build a plane?

Given the chance, what would you build? What comments would you make about the illustrations in this book? Are they sufficiently detailed to actually enable you to build a model of the plane?

Activity

The last picture in the book includes four posters about space travel. Imagine you are building a lunar module out of things around your home; draw plans of what it would look like.

Read *The sea people* by Muller.

Discuss

Compare the illustrations on the first double-page spread, at the height of the storm, and the last pages of the book; what differences do you notice?
Look carefully at the way in which the artist has drawn people's faces; what emotions are conveyed?
Compare the lifestyle on both islands; how do they differ?
What action by the King on the Greater Island led to its destruction?
In the last double-page spread a large ship is being built; where do you think it will be sailed to?

Activity

Draw a map showing the two islands and

the route which the ship will take on its journey.

Paint a large mural illustrating both islands; list beneath each island words that you feel describe the life style of the people living there.

Read *Blackbeard the pirate* by Ambrus.

Activity

This is a book to read with a friend. As children read, suggest they compile a list of the 'play on words' that Ambrus has used. Follow this up with children illustrating their own 'play on words' display. Draw a pirate map which details the sequence that takes place in the story.

Read *Dracula* by Ambrus as a follow-up.

Read *The bear who wanted to stay a bear* by Jorg Muller.

Discuss

Select topics from the following suggestions:

What does the title tell us about the content of the story?

Where do you think the story is set?

What time of the year is it at the start?

What descriptive words are used to create visual images of the season/s?

Discuss the mood of the first three illustrations.

Does the author make us feel good or bad about the factory being built? How?

How did the bear feel when he woke up? (imitate/mime)

What was his first experience of the factory?

Why did he act as he did?

Discuss the sequence of events as he becomes 'humanized'.

Are the human characters shown as good or bad? Discuss dialogue and illustrations.

What were the implications of no-one believing he was a 'real' bear? (e.g. illustrations of Chairman and bear rug; zoo; circus)

How did the bear feel as he became a worker?

How do *you* feel watching the process?

In what ways did he change, if any?

Discuss the illustrations of the inside of the factory.

Compare with similar situations in our society.

How does this compare with a 'natural' existence?

What began to take effect as autumn drew on?

Compare illustrations of the bear falling asleep on the job, with those earlier of him waking from hibernation.

Why did the bear go to a motel?

What happened?

What was the 'something important' he almost forgot?

How did you feel about the ending?

What techniques did the illustrator use to achieve this effect?

Can you suggest an alternate ending?

Can you suggest why the author wrote this story? What does he want us to think about? (i.e. theme and intentions)

Did the story demonstrate the title?

Do you have any criticisms? (e.g. dialogue, plot, characters, illustrations)

What other books by this author have you read?

Are the themes similar? How?

Activity

Children could write cinquain verse/full verse, about bears, hibernation, industrialization, seasons, etc. Design a cover for the book.

Read *The sparrow's story at the King's command*, discovered by Judith Crabtree (Oxford University Press).

Discuss

Is the story written by the King's scribes the same as the one originally written by the storyteller?
How has the story changed?
Who changes or adds to the story?
Look at the book's title page; is the book written by Judith Crabtree?
What does all this mean? (The dedication may give you a clue).
What do you notice about the last illustration and the book that has just been read to you?

In the top left-hand corner of the first illustration three butcher-birds are watching the storyteller. Where else do they appear?
What period of history is represented in the story?
Do you think this influenced the style of illustration used by the author?

Activity

The first letter on each page is illuminated and each illustration has a decorative border. Look at these carefully and notice how they match the story.
Design a poster, using decorative borders and illuminated letters, to advertise the book.

A POETRY STARTER

Read a poem a day

Poetry is meant to be read aloud. Have plenty of short informal sessions where you and the children 'dip into' poetry. Expose children to a wide variety of poetry forms and types; one-letter poems, counting/skipping rhymes, tongue-twisters, shape poems, poems by children, humorous poems, poems about feelings, haiku, ballads, limericks, cinquain, free verse, poems about space, ghosts and other topics.

Choose poems that are meaningful to the children; don't play safe and select only traditional verse.

Create a poetry climate by
- placing posters on walls advertising poems on a particular topic
- building up class scrap-books of poetry discoveries encouraging children to build up personal poetry collections
- holding poetry-of-the-week competitions
- having children read poetry to each other.

Beware of overemphasizing analysis and memorizing of poetry; both have a place, but in small doses.

A starting point: Poetry themes

Provide children with a poetry diet which includes different forms and types. Poetry themes provide a framework in which this can be achieved.

The following framework, which can be applied to any group of poems, deals with four humorous selections from Shel Silverstein's *Where the sidewalk ends* and introduces children to the concept of cautionary verse.

1. The poems could be read in a half-hour session, or throughout one day.
2. Pre-read the poems to decide appropriate speed, voice, loudness and rhythm.
3. Start by discussing the concept of cautionary verse, i.e. poems which contain warnings/lessons.
4. Ask children to listen to the selected poems and decide what the warning is in each one.
5. Read the poem/s.
6. Discuss answers to the question above, highlighting the humorous way in which the warnings are given.
7. Follow up with appropriate activities, if interest warrants.

The four Silverstein poems are: 'Warning', 'Jimmy Jet', 'Boa-constrictor' and 'The gypsies are coming', in *Where the sidewalk ends*.

Activities and discussion points

'Warning' (p. 75)
Did you find the poem frightening or not? Why?
Do you think hearing this poem would actually make you change the habit it talks about?
Read H. Belloc's verse about the Scissor Man in 'Struwwelpeter'.

'Jimmy Jet' (p. 28)
Survey children's TV-watching habits.

Examine the rhyming structure of the poem; compare with 'Warning'.
Perhaps extend into rhyming activities, for example, rhyming word games: supply second and fourth rhyming lines, children to add first and third.

'Boa-constrictor' (p. 45)
Children chant poem after the first reading.
Read other chants from *Juba this and Juba that* by Tashjian.
Reproduce the illustration of the boa in large format, and display; look at and make other 'shape' poems.

'The Gypsies are coming' (p. 50)
Contrast rhyming techniques with those used in 'Jimmy Jet'.
Children join in chant; perhaps use drum or other percussion instrument to emphasize rhythm.
Read other poems about gypsies, e.g. 'My mother said, I never should, play with the gypsies in the wood . . .'.

Try these poetry activities

Make a 'poet tree' — shapes of fruit and leaves carry poems.
A world trip through poetry, introducing verse from various countries.
Feature an object (toy, flower) with a poster poem.
Hold a poetry feast — poems about things to eat.
Collect seasonal poems and display with suitable pictures.

Make a poetry zoo — cut-out animal shapes carry poems.
Make a giant cat, and cover with cat poems.
Poetry mobiles.
Window poems — paint directly on to windows or plastic sheets.
Poetry mural — poems on one theme stretching across wall.
Poetry cards from publishers, or make your own.
Poetry to music, and poems that are songs, for example, 'I know an old lady who swallowed a fly'; 'Morning has broken', Cat Stevens song based on the poem by Eleanor Farjeon.

Bibliography

Collections of Contemporary Poetry

Allen, J. *A bad case of animal nonsense* (Godine)

Clark, L. *The singing time* (Hodder & Stoughton)

—— *The way the wind blows* (Evans)

Cole, W. *Beastly boys and ghastly girls* (Methuen)

Dugan, M. *More stuff and nonsense* (Collins)

—— *My old dad and other funny things like him* (Longman Cheshire)

Foster, J. *A second poetry book* (Oxford University Press)

Giles, B. *My animal friends* (Longman Cheshire)

—— *People and places* (Longman Cheshire)

—— *Wind sky and wings* (Longman Cheshire)

—— *I like the town* (Longman Cheshire)

Hughes, T. *Meet my folks* (Faber/Puffin)

Ireson, B. *Beaver book of funny rhymes* (Beaver Books/Hamlyn)

Katz, B. *Upside down and inside out* (Watts)

Macleod, D. *Hippopotabus* (Outback Press)

—— *In the garden of bad things* (Kestrel/Puffin)

—— *The story of Admiral Sneeze* (Kingfisher)

Milligan, S. *Goblins* (Arrow Books)

—— *Unspun socks from a chicken's laundry* (M. Joseph/M. & J. Hobbs)

Moore, L. *See my lovely poison ivy* (Atheneum)

Oliver, R. S. *Cornucopia* (Atheneum)

Osborn, V. *One big yo to go* (Oxford University Press)

Patten, B. *The sly cormorant and the fishes* (Allen & Unwin)

Prelutsky, J. *Nightmares* (Black, UK; Greenwillow, USA)

—— *The headless horseman rides again* (Greenwillow)

Rosen, M. *Mind your own business* (Armada Lions/Deutsch)

Saunders, D. *Weathers and seasons* (Evans)

Silverstein, S. *A light in the attic (Cape)*

—— *Where the sidewalk ends* (Harper & Row)

Thompson, B. *Lollipops* (Longman Young)

Thwaite, A. *All sorts of poems* (Magnet Books/Methuen)

Wallace, D. *Giant poems* (Holiday House)

—— *Monster poems* (Holiday House)

—— *Witch poems* (Holiday House)

BOOK TALKS

Introducing book talks

Begin by allowing each child *only* 30 seconds to talk about a book to the class or group.

Encourage and develop self-criticism of the presentation.

Allow the audience to praise and criticize constructively, i.e. have the presenters ask themselves

Did I repeat myself?

Did I make long pauses?

Did I um! and ah!?

Gradually extend the time of the presentation.

As each extension of time is made, teach by demonstration how to add further elements to the book talks.

Time	Content
30 seconds	Author, title, illustrator, main character, one idea or theme of the story.
60 seconds	As above, plus where the story takes place and a description of this setting.
75 seconds	As above, and introduce minor characters. Outline the plot leading to the climax.
90 seconds	As above, plus details of role played by characters and their relationships with one another.
2 minutes	As above, and continue to add details of plot, theme, mood and personal responses to the story.

An alternative

Place a 30–60-second limit on the talk, but specify the aspect of the discussion, for example,

40 seconds to tell only about characters,

or

40 seconds to describe the settings used by the author,

or

60 seconds to read an exceptionally good descriptive passage.

Children should be encouraged to talk confidently about books in an atmosphere of mutual trust, and respect for opinions.

BOOK DISCUSSION GROUPS

It is crucial that children aged 10–12 be given many opportunities, both informally and formally, to discuss the literature they are reading. Such discussions with peers and adults (teachers/parents) will help children to achieve the abilities listed in the framework on pages 74 and 75. The following approaches formalize literature discussion among students, via book discussion groups. Whichever approach is used, start in a small way with one/two groups; if interest warrants and adult leaders are available, expand the programme to include more groups and other age groups.

Approach 1

Contract reading

1 Children form friendship groups and choose a novel from sets of multiple copies available (groups consist of five students and an adult leader).
2 The groups approach any teacher/parent participating in the scheme and draw up a contract. (This should be easy if you are starting with only one/two groups).

```
Contract
We _____; _____
_____; _____
agree to read _____ (title)
by _____ (author)
and on _____ (date)
at _____ (time) will hold a book
discussion with (parent/teacher.)
```

3 Most of the reading is done in the children's own time, although teachers could allocate some of their timetabled reading sessions for contract reading.
4 The group meets with an adult to discuss their chosen novel (See list of possible book discussion questions on page 96).

Variations on Approach 1

Instead of reading the chosen novel alone, children and teacher could have sessions of group-reading, aloud. This is particularly valuable for less able readers.

Approach 2

Individualized reading

1 Each child is provided with a suggested reading list for his or her grade level.
2 Books are selected from multiple-copy sets by individual children.
3 Children read the chosen novel in their own time.
4 As each child completes their novel they indicate, on a master timetable, that they are ready for a discussion.
5 When sufficient children have completed the same novel, groups are formed with an adult leader.
   Note: This approach requires that many adults are available as leaders.

Book discussion questions

Obviously not all these questions need be asked at each discussion session; one question may stimulate a full discussion.

Characterization

Who were the main characters?
What were they like? (physical description)
What type of person were they?
Did you like/dislike them?
Why were they important to the story?
Why did they behave as they did?
Was it good/bad behaviour?
Do you know anyone like them?
How did they change throughout the story?

Setting

Where did the story take place?
What was the place like?
Could there be a place like this?
Would you like to live there?
When did the story take place? (past, present, future)
Was there, or could there be a time like this?

Mood

How did you feel while reading the story?
What was the saddest/funniest incident?
What was the most exciting/unusual/ mysterious incident?
How did the author make you feel the way you did?
What do you remember most about the story?

Plot

What happened in the story? (Verbalize sequence of events.)

What might have happened if a certain action had not ended as it did?
What other way might the story have ended?

Style

Was the book easy to read?
Did the author use simple words?
Were there any unusual ways of saying things?

Theme

Why do you think the author wrote the book?
What is the author trying to make us think about?
What do we learn about the author's thinking?

Form

Was this story
  real
  fantasy
  legend
  folklore
  biography
  history?

Book certificates

Certificates awarded for books which have been completed, read and discussed, provide an incentive for future reading. An example of an award certificate can be found on page 97. This certificate may be freely copied. There is space on the certificate for teachers to write in the number of books read, for example, the certificate printed on blue paper could be for 5 books; the certificate on red for 10; a gold certificate for 20.

This

Certificate

is awarded to

_____

who has read _____

_____

and participated in a literature

discussion

LITERATURE AWARD

Signed _____

Date _____

BOOK STUDIES – FICTION

Introduction:

The books listed below are suitable for serial reading to children at this level. While it is not the authors' intention that all of the following activities be undertaken for each book, the studies do provide opportunity for children to interact with literature through writing, drawing and discussion.
It is the teacher's role to choose those activities which are best suited to the children's interests and abilities.
In the course of serial reading, it may only be appropriate to introduce activities for one or two chapters.
Finally, the approach taken with these studies may be applied to other novels.

Mrs Frisby and the rats of Nimh by Robert O'Brien; *Dragon slayer* by Rosemary Sutcliff; *The turbulent term of Tyke Tiler* by Gene Kemp; *The midnight fox* by Betsy Byars; *The boy who was afraid* by Armstrong Sperry.

Mrs Frisby and the rats of Nimh
by Robert C. O'Brien

This book is to be read as a serial daily with ongoing periodic activities.
Read Chapters 1 and 2 as the introduction.

Activity

Staple several sheets of paper together as pages for a booklet.
Attach cover.
'We are going to make our own Mrs Frisby booklet and work in it from time to time as we read the serial'.
Design cover.
Include author, title, publisher.

Discuss

Explain the Newbery Medal and talk about it.

Continue daily reading sessions slotting in the following activities.

Activities

Reserve one page as a picture gallery of the main characters. Add to it as characters assume importance or as new characters are met.

Read the description of Mrs Frisby's
house in Chapter 1 and have the children
draw their pictorial interpretation of the
house.

After Chapters 1–3, children draw a map
of Mrs Frisby's house in relation to the
rest of the farm.
Include:
   farm house
   barn
   rosebush
   fields to be ploughed
   the woods
   Mr Age's House.
Perhaps a 'bird's eye' view could be
taken.

Vocabulary

Divide one or two pages for recording
word lists.

Describing characters	*Action words*
How characters felt nervous foolish agitated bewildered puzzled affectionate	*Describing places*

Listening

Children may be asked to listen for a
specific group type during different
listening sessions.
After Chapter 16
   Draw or construct a model maze.
   Play maze games.
   Discuss mazes for humans.

Related story

'Theseus and the Minotaur'

Discuss

Following each chapter, have a
discussion which will highlight
a the anticipation of outcomes
b prediction of events
c comparison of characters
d relationships between preceding and
   subsequent events
e author's feelings for his character
f listener's emotional reactions to
   characters/events
g how human characteristics are related
   to the behaviour and feelings of animal
   characters
h causes for the behaviour of characters.

Write cinquain (san-kane) for main characters.

Dragon	1 word — Title
Enormous cat	2 words — Describe the title
Creeping, crushing, hunter	3 words — Describe movement
Fierce enemy of mice	4 words — Words express feelings
Monster	1 word — Synonym

Acrostic writing
Resourceful
Articulate
Trained
Secretive

Organized
Friendly

Notable
Intelligent
Mature
Helpful

SOCK PUPPET

Classification of vocabulary under the following headings:
human characters
animal characters
friendly characters
unfriendly characters
safe settings
unsafe settings
humorous events
exciting events
frightening events.

Think about rats.
Many people fear rats as dirty, disease-ridden and dangerous.
How has reading about Mrs Frisby and the rats of Nimh changed or confirmed your thoughts?

Discuss

Debate the use of rats for laboratory experiments.

Activities

Make a crossword puzzle for the story.

Make a 'filmstrip'.
One 'frame' can be drawn for each chapter.

Make bookmarks of the characters from the story.

Using simple handicraft books for instructions, make finger, glove or stick puppets of the characters.
Use these for vocabulary work.
Be the character of the puppet and introduce yourself to the group.

Write 'Who am I?' quiz questions.

Play '20 Questions' to discover the name of the character, a setting or an event.
Rules — one child decides on a character, setting or event and writes this on a slip of paper. The remainder of the grade may ask 20 questions which are phrased so that they elicit only a yes/no answer.

Make a game

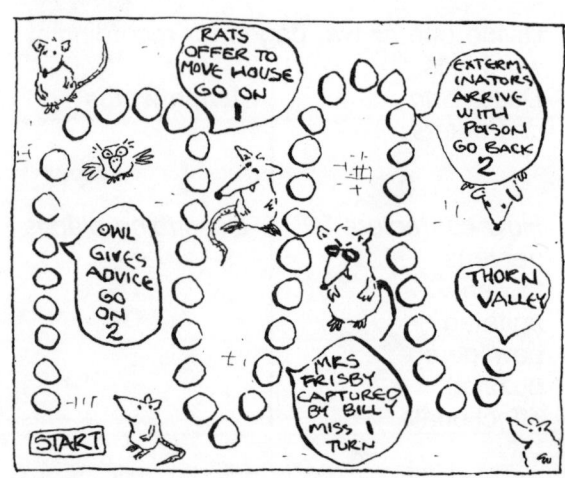

Discuss

Which part of the story do you think the author enjoyed writing most?
Which character do you think he liked/disliked most?
What do you think he thought about rats?

Some other stories about rats and mice: Burman, Ben Lucian, *High water at Cat Fish Bend*; Cleary, Beverly, *The mouse and the motorcycle* and *Runaway Ralph*; Selden, George, *Cricket in Times Square*; Sharp, Margery, *Miss Bianca* and *The rescuers*; White E. B. *Stuart Little*.

This book has been made into an animated film called 'The secret of Nimh'.

Dragon slayer

by Rosemary Sutcliff

It is suggested that Chapters 1 and 2 be paraphrased by the teacher. Tell the story in your own language to explain clearly the relationships between characters and to provide background information about Vikings and their life style.

Chapter 3

Vocabulary

List and discuss words associated with food and drink; transportation; clothing.

Use a dictionary to determine meaning of unfamiliar words.

Discuss

Talk about the jester, Hunferth, and his role at court.

Research

Use encyclopedia to research background information on jesters.

Locate geographical setting of the story.

Discuss

What was Hunferth's reaction to Beowulf. Why should he feel this way?

Retelling

Retell the story of Beowulf and Breca and the search for the walrus.

Chapter 4

Discuss

What are the powers possessed by Grendel?
What other 'creatures' do you know that are man-eaters?

Related stories

'Theseus and the Minotaur'
'Ulysses and the Cyclops'

Activities

Write an eyewitness news report of the coming of Grendel and the fight between Beowulf and the monster.
Design newspaper headlines for the event.
Use some of the alternative names given for Grendel: Night Stalker, Death Shadow.
Using a black pencil, draw Grendel.

Discuss

How do you think news was reported and stored in Anglo-Saxon times?
The role of the Bard:

- storyteller
- carrier of news
- holder of the tribe's traditional knowledge and history.

Chapter 5

Discuss

Grendel arrives home.
What do you think happened between mother and son?
How do they communicate?
Instinct and emotion: what is the difference?
Why was the Sea-Hag more terrible for being able to love?

Where was Grendel's father?
What was he?
Why did Grendel's mother kidnap rather than rampage and kill?

Activity

Write further news reports of the new terror.
Make use of various expressions referring to the creature:
    Death Shadow in the Dark
    Wolf Woman
    Sea Hag
Make up other descriptive phrases.

Discuss

Discuss Beowulf's statement, 'It is better that a man avenge his friend than mourn him overmuch' (page 56).
Look at the simile used on page 59,
'. . . lying abandoned like some fragment of a mouse that a great cat has dropped from its jaws.'
Discuss other similes and in a language session create some original similes.

Chapter 6

Activity

Illustrate a series of pictures of the battle,
    or
the story so far,
    or
a mural of the story,
    or
silhouettes of the characters,
    or
a cross-section of the underwater cave of the Sea-Hag,
    or
Grendel's territory, using appropriate colours, and referring to the description on page 58.

Vocabulary

List words to describe this place: the lights, sounds, and tides.
Make up a story that people might tell about the place.

Discuss

Talk about the change of heart by the Jester, Hunferth, and his gift to Beowulf.
Why does he now like Beowulf?
What is the relationship between Grendel and the walruses?
Why did they leave after the battle between Beowulf and the Sea-Hag?

Related story

The sword is named Hrunting.
What other sword has a name?
Read about Excalibur and King Arthur.

Chapter 7

Activities

Compose the song that the Bard in Hrothgar's court may have sung about the slaying of Grendel and his mother by Beowulf.

As a group, re-enact the farewell to

Beowulf from Hrothgar's hall, the loading and then the launching of the boat.

Make a model of Beowulf's boat.

Chapter 8

Discuss

How was time recorded, in terms of seasons and migration cycles? Use this method to tell your age.
How old is Beowulf? (page 85)
How long is the dragon? (page 86)
Devise your own measurement system using seasonal clues, for example:

    39 times had he heard the cicadas whistling in the month of his birth.
    Q. How old is the man?
    Q. What month was he born?
    Q. What year was he born?

Chapter 9

Activities

Illustrate as a wall frieze the confrontation with the dragon,
    or
add a further panel to the wall mural started earlier.

Acrostics
    Brave warrior
    Exciting hero
    Ousted Grendel
    Wise leader
    Unbeaten in battle
    Liberator
    Faithful friend

Compile others using descriptive phrases for Grendel, The Dragon and other important characters.

Discuss

What is the significance of the sword's disintegration as Beowulf dies.
Compare this with the return of King Arthur's Excalibur to the lake.
As Beowulf, describe your feelings as you are confronted by the dragon.
What were the burial rites used in Anglo-Saxon times.
Compare these to other monuments, pyramids, and modern tombstones.
How would the people remember Beowulf?
What did they fear after his death? Why?
Compose an epitaph to Beowulf.

Activity

Compile a 'Code of behavior' for a Viking Warrior.
What was expected?
What characteristics did they find honorable?

Related story

'St. George and the Dragon'

The turbulent term of Tyke Tiler
by Gene Kemp
Chapter 1

Discuss

Who are the most interesting characters so far?
Why do you think Tyke helps Danny?
How do you think Danny and Tyke became friends?
Should Tyke have hidden the money?
What do you think will happen next?

Activities

Write a short account of the day Tyke met Danny for the first time.
Say where and how they met.

Chapter 2

Discuss

Why did Chief Sir suspect Tyke of hiding the money?
Do you think the punishment that Tyke and Danny received was fair?

Activities

Draw a cartoon of the mouse's escape at assembly; supply a suitable caption.

Chapter 4

Discuss

Where do you think the story is taking place?
Which country?
What type of area: urban/rural?

What words and phrases do the characters use which helped you decide this?
Is Tyke's school like yours or different? How?

Activity

Look at the text and make a list of words that the characters use and which are new to you. Write a meaning for each.

Chapter 5

Discuss

How was Danny's reaction to the secret hiding place different from Tyke's?
This hiding place becomes important later in the story; predict how it might be used by Danny and Tyke.

Activity

How has the author made the old mill seem spooky?
Look at the description in the book and select those words which give this spooky feeling.

Chapter 6

Discuss

Would you enjoy being in Tyke's grade? Why?
Have you noticed the riddles that begin each chapter?
Why do you think they are there?

Activity

Many of the characters have been given nicknames.
List them and write a short sentence next to each one, telling why the name has been given.

Chapter 7

Discuss

What prompted Tyke to steal the test?
What do you think will happen next?
How would you describe the story so far: humorous, sad, exciting, boring?

Activity

Write a police report of the vandalism at Tyke's school.
There have been several major incidents in the story so far; draw two of these.

Chapter 8

Activity

Look at the illustration on page 78.
Describe the conversation that is taking place between Tyke and Danny.
You've met most of the characters in the story by now.
Classify them according to whether they are liked or disliked by Tyke. Draw a picture of Tyke and list these characters underneath using the headings 'Likes' and 'Dislikes'.

Chapter 10

Discuss

By now you will have realized that Tyke and Danny are good friends. What are the things that you think are important in friendships?

Activity

Write an advertisement asking for a friend.
Describe the friend's appearance and what qualities the friend should have.

Chapter 11

Discuss

Tyke originally stole the test to help Danny. How has the plan back-fired? What would you do, if you were Tyke, to put things right between you and Danny?

Activity

As a group, draw a map of the story's setting; show all the places where major events have taken place.

Chapter 12

Discuss

Where do you think Danny has run away to?
At this stage, people in Tyke's house seem to be upset.
What things cause upsets or arguments in your house?

Chapter 14

Discuss

How did you feel when you found out that Tyke was a girl?
How did the author manage to keep this a secret?
If you suspected, what clues helped you?
Does it change your feelings about the story and Tyke? If so, how?

Activity

Write to the author care of the publisher.
Read *Gowie Corby plays chicken* also by Gene Kemp.

The midnight fox
by Betsy Byars

Chapter 1

Discuss

How did Tom's parents try to change his mind about not wanting to go to the farm?
How would you describe Tom: selfish?

Activity

List the statements used in Chapter 1 by Tom's parents to persuade him to go to the farm.

Chapter 4

Discuss

Have Tom's feelings about the farm changed now that he's there?
The tree outside Tom's window becomes important later in the story. Can you predict how?

Chapter 5

Discuss

What were Tom's reactions when he sighted the fox?

Activity

Make a list of words and phrases used by the author to describe the fox.
Pretend you are Tom; write a letter to Petie about discovering the black fox.

Write short descriptions which summarize your feelings about each of the characters met so far in the story.

Chapter 6

Discuss

Why does Tom keep his sighting of the fox a secret?
In what ways does Tom's view about the fox differ from his uncle's?

Activity

Compare the lifestyles of Tom's parents with that of Aunt Millie's family.

Chapter 8

Discuss

How did Tom feel as he followed the fox into the forest?
Why is he reluctant to let his uncle know about the fox?
Does Hazeline feel the same as Tom, or her father, about foxes?

Activity

Draw a map showing the farm and forest. As the story progresses mark in any details which the author reveals about the fox's territory.

Chapter 9

Discuss

Why is Tom ill at ease with his uncle?

Activity

Make a list of
- Tom's fears that have been revealed so far
- the things which Tom has discovered about foxes.

List some of your fears.
Tom's friend Petie has a habit of summing up situations via newspaper headlines. Make up a headline which summarizes Tom's feelings about the fox.

Chapter 10

Discuss

What do you think is going to happen that will cause Tom to go back to the den?

Activity

Add the location of the fox's den to your map.
Tom is obviously very involved with the fox and its lifestyle. Use books or an encyclopedia to find out more about foxes.

Chapter 13

Discuss

In this chapter Tom and his uncle exhibit different emotions about the fox. What are these?
How do you think Tom can prevent his uncle from locating the fox's den?

Chapter 16

Discuss

Tom reveals to Hazeline his feelings about the fox.
How does she respond?
How does Tom react to the baby fox's cry for its mother?
Why do you think the author connects this event to that of Petie breaking his leg?

Chapter 17

Discuss

How does Tom's uncle react, when he discovers that Tom has let the baby fox escape?
Does his reaction change Tom's opinion of him? How?

Chapter 19

Discuss

In what ways has Tom's attitude to the farm changed?
Do you feel Tom has overcome any of his fears? Which ones?

The boy who was afraid
by Armstrong Sperry

Chapters 1 and 2

Discuss

What has been the most dramatic event so far.

Predict what you think will happen to Mafatu.

Activity

Compile a list of Polynesian words used in the text.
Encourage students to scan the text to discover the meanings of the words, for example:

    purau — type of timber
    tupa pau — ghost spirit

Add to this list as the story progresses.

Chapter 3

Discuss

What aspects of Polynesian culture have you discovered so far.
Aspects may include
- roles of boys, women, men
- food — types, how it is gathered
- transport — canoe making
- religion — discuss tabu, why the island is a sacred place
- arts — music, stories, costume and jewellery
- Mafatu's life — his fears, his responsibilities, his loneliness.

What do you fear in your life?
Have you ever felt great loneliness?
What responsibilities do you have to your family and community?
How have you had to prove yourself to your friends/family?

Chapter 5

Activity

Using the information in Chapter 3 design a map of the island on the outline provided on page 111.
Before starting, design your own symbols for each of the features.

Introduce *Island of the blue dolphins* by O'Dell.
Read the following three extracts which treat problems similar to those faced by Mafatu.
1 Chapter 12 deals with Karana developing survival skills.
2 The end of Chapter 16 tells of the sighting of an octopus.
3 In Chapter 19 Karana hunts the octopus.
Discuss the similarities/differences between the experiences of Mafatu and Karana.

Activities

Make a model of Mafatu's island. Base it on the mapping work done after Chapter 5.

Make a model of the outrigger canoe; use cardboard or balsa wood.

Try dyeing your own material. Use plant dyes: an easy one to start — brown onion skins.

Related story

Robinson Crusoe by Defoe (particularly Crusoe's encounter with cannibals)

Activity

A crossword puzzle to be answered using Polynesian words from the text is included on page 110.

Bibliography

Use the following books to develop a theme concerned with an individual's survival and overcoming fear.

Byars, Betsy *The 18th emergency* (Bodley Head/Puffin)
Cormier, Robert *The chocolate war* (Armada Books/Gollancz)
DeFoe, Daniel *Robinson Crusoe* (Penguin)
DeJong, Mindert *The house of 60 fathers* (Puffin)
Hautzig, Esther *The endless steppe* (Hamish Hamilton)
Holm, Anne *I am David* (Methuen)
Mattingley, Christobel *Windmill at Magpie Creek* (Hodder)
O'Dell, Scott *Island of the blue dolphins* (Kestrel)
Southall, Ivan *Let the balloon go* (Penguin)
Taylor, Theodore *The cay* (Puffin)

Crossword puzzle

Polynesian words from *The boy who was afraid.*

(Scan the text of the story to locate the appropriate word.)

1 Clothing made of bark (Ch. 2)
2 A sacred place (Ch. 3)
3 A large sea-bird (Ch. 1)
4 Eaters-of-men (Ch. 4)
5 Island chestnut-trees (two words) (Ch. 3)
6 A quality worshipped by the Polynesians (Ch. 1)
7 The race of people (Ch. 1)
8 Wild bananas (Ch. 3)
9 Wild (Ch. 4)

10 The ghost spirit (Ch. 1)
11 Ancient words for Pacific Ocean currents (two words) (Ch. 2)
12 The god of fishermen (Ch. 2)
13 Sudden gusts of wind (Ch. 2)
14 Octopus (Ch. 4)
15 Tree used to make a canoe (Ch. 1)
16 Name of Mafatu's dog (Ch. 1)
17 Framework projecting from the side of the canoe (Ch. 1)
18 A means of sea transport
19 Giant clam (Ch. 5)
20 Pig (Ch. 4)
21 Forbidden Island (two words) (Ch. 3)
22 Violent storm (Ch. 1)

Mapping exercise
The boy who was afraid

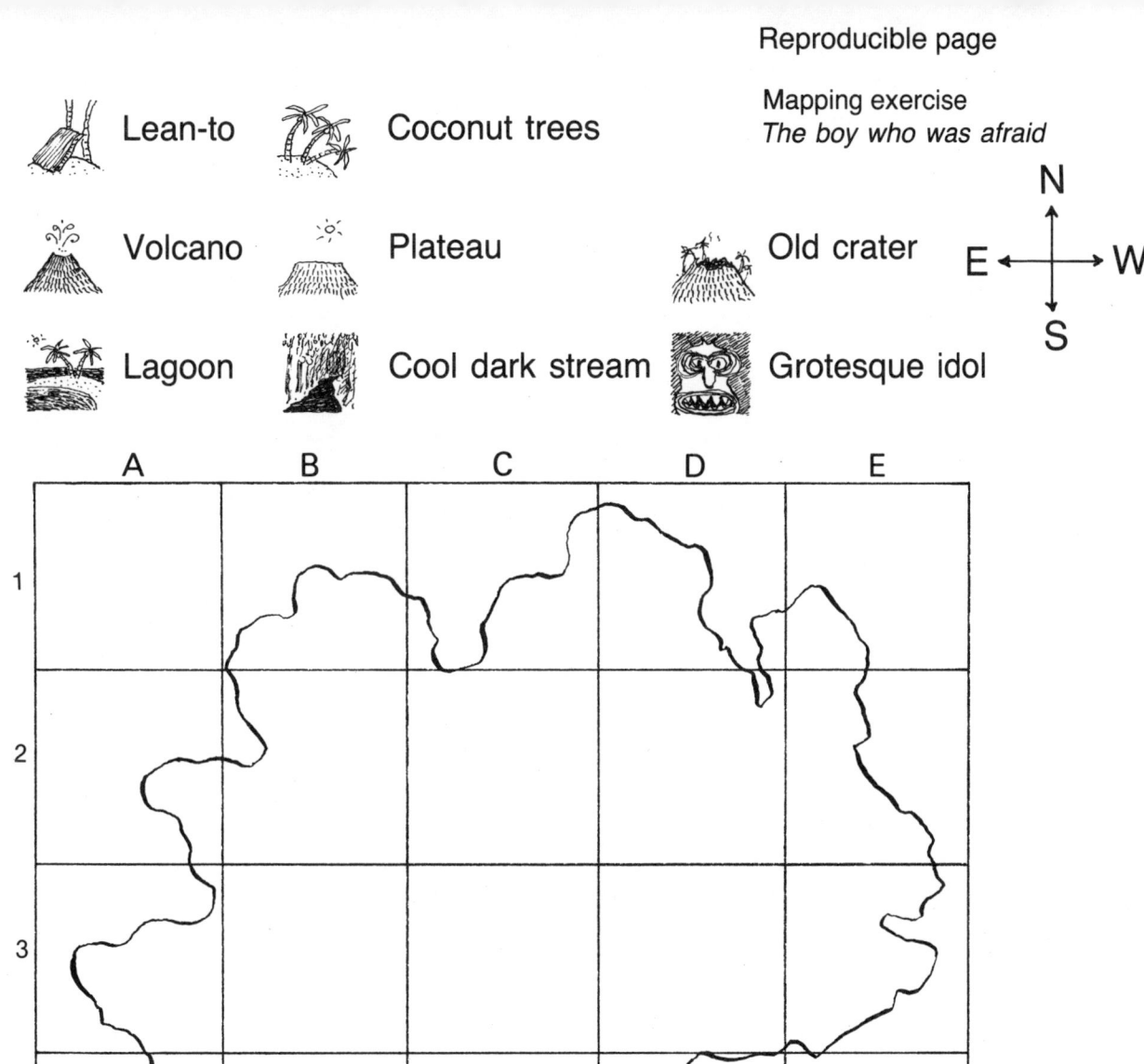

Appendices

Book reports

Remember that a book review or report is to be read by others. Display reviews and encourage children to read them to each other. In the early stages of learning to write a report, provide clear guidelines as to what you expect the report will contain. Suggest formats for the reports and vary the presentations.

The skills involved in writing a book report should be developed in stages throughout the child's school life. See the outline for book talks on p. 94. Increase the complexity of the written reports along similar lines.

A book report *need not* be written for every book read. Limit the number of reports required to two, or at the most three, per term.

Encourage variety in the presentation. The following reproducible pages outline three possible book report formats.

My name _____

Title _____

Author _____

Call number _____

1 Is this story true?   Yes ☐ No ☐ (tick one)

2 This book is about: (tick one)

Animals ☐   Mystery ☐

Science ☐   Adventure ☐

3 Which person did you like best?

_____

4 Name a character you did not like.

_____

5 Was the book funny?   Yes ☐ No ☐

6 What place does the book tell about?

_____

7 Would other children like the book?

_____

Why/Why not? _____

My name   _____

Book title   _____

Author's name   _____

    Tick one box in each column.

This book:

☐   is a good book

☐   I didn't like it

☐   is not interesting

☐   is too hard

☐   is just right

☐   is too easy

☐   had no pictures

☐   had good pictures

☐   had too many pictures

This is

_____

This is

_____

the character I liked most.

where some of the story took place.

Title _____

Author _____

Draw pictures in each of the boxes.

The place where the story started

The most important character

The most exciting event that happened
to the most important character

How the story ended

A cryptic book-title quiz

Make large display cards by copying the following representations of book titles. Display them prominently for a literature competition in which children match titles to appropriate pictures.

The black stallion

Blue fin

Dot and the kangaroo

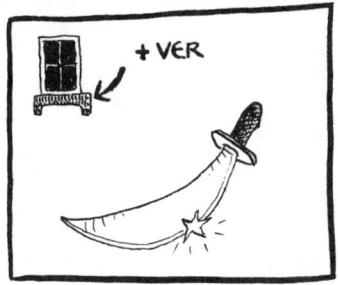

The silver sword

Ten apples up on top

The tiger in the teapot

New blue shoes

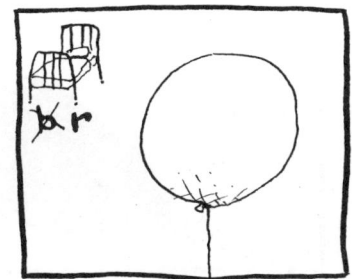

The red balloon

Goldilocks

Seven little Australians

Black Jack

Asterix

Half magic

My side of the mountain

Alice in Wonderland

Tiger's milk

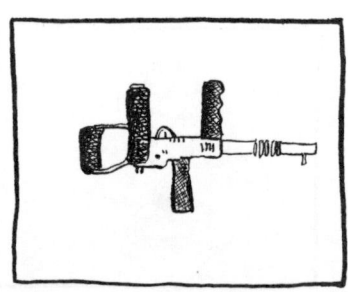

The machine gunners

The lion the witch and the wardrobe

The 13 clocks

Greensmoke

Tongue-twisters and Knock-knocks

Session 1

Begin with a competition of saying tongue-twisters. (Present them on prepared cards.)

Introduce books which contain tongue-twisters.

Swap known knock-knocks with the group.

Read some of the 'cryptic' type knock-knocks from 'Junior voices' and 'Voices'. Encourage group members to illustrate the tongue-twisters and knock-knock cards that were represented; make up others as they are offered by the children.

File these cards for future reading or tongue-twister competitions. Leave them in a box, readily accessible for all to read and practise at any time.

Session 2

Discuss

How is a tongue-twister constructed?
What is alliteration?
Demonstrate its use in poetry by reading examples.

Encourage children individually or with a partner to compose an 'original' tongue-twister.

They are to write it on a card, illustrate it, practise saying it and present it to the group at the end of the session.

Session 3

Extend the notion of a single sentence containing words beginning with the same letter, to a set of sentences which tell a story.

Activity

Make up an 'L story' or an 'O story'.

Begin this activity as a brainstorming session with the class. All can contribute to the first couple of stories.

The first stories may only be two or three sentences long but with practice, they can be extended.

Provide a starting phrase:
'Five fat frogs flopped . . .'
'Old Oscar of Ouyen often . . .'

Allow individuals or groups of children to create their own single-letter stories.

Display the stories on large letters cut from coloured card.

Counting-out rhymes

Session 1

Encourage children to discuss the rhymes they use to count while skipping or choosing who's to be in or out of a game. For example:

> One potato, two potato
> three potato, four
> five potato, six potato
> seven potato, more.
> or
> Red top taxi, 1, 2, 3
> Red top taxi
> You're not he.

Chant some of the well known rhymes. Discuss the age of the chants, those that are thought to be old. Why?
How do we tell a new chant?
Illustrate the chants on paper to make a 'chant collection book' for the library.
Encourage children to survey parents, aunts, uncles, and grandparents about the chants they remember from childhood.

Session 2

Compare chants remembered by other family members.
Illustrate any 'new' ones and add them to the collection started in Session 1.
Show books which contain rhymes.
Play games which involve chants.
Introduce this chant and say it as a round.

> Ah-hem Ah-hem
> Me mother has gone to church
> She says I'm not to play with you
> Because you're in the dirt.
>
> It isn't because you're dirty
> It isn't because you're clean
> It's because you've got the whooping cough
> And eat margarine.

What are these colours? — shades of
                                what colour?
ultramarine
crimson
navy
shocking
emerald
scarlet
primrose
lilac
sepia
royal
ochre
buttercup
buff
leaf
eau-de-nil
prussian
maroon
ivory

as (red) as a beetroot
(green) with envy
Rhythm and (blues)
(white) wedding
(green) fingers
in the (pink)
(black) as the ace of spades
feeling (blue)
like a (red) rag to a bull
every cloud has a (silver) lining
(yellow) i.e. cowardly
(red) i.e. labour
(blue) i.e. Conservative
(yellow/orange) i.e. ~~Lib/Lab~~ Alliance
(rose) coloured spectacles.
out of the (blue)

Questions for literature games

Which animal?	Title
Ping (duck)	*The story of Ping*
Old Yella (dog)	*Old Yella*
Fish Head (cat)	*Fish Head*
Bambi (fawn)	*Bambi*
Yertle (turtle)	*Yertle the Turtle*
Sounder (dog)	*Sounder*
Mrs Frisby (mouse)	*Mrs Frisby and the rats of Ninmh*
Miss Bianca (mouse)	*Miss Bianca*
Ribsy (dog)	*Henry Huggins*
Bagheera (panther) } Baloo (bear) Shere Khan (tiger) }	*The Mowgli stories* by Rudyard Kipling
Pongo (dalmation)	*101 dalmations*
Mr Percival (pelican)	*Storm Boy*
Tarka (otter)	*Tarka the otter*
Black Beauty (horse)	*Black Beauty*
Moby Dick (whale)	*Moby Dick*
Horton (elephant)	*Horton hatches the egg*
Charlotte (spider) } Wilbur (pig) Templeton (rat) }	*Charlotte's web* by E. B. White
Ralph (mouse)	*The mouse and the motorcyle*
Lassie (dog)	*Lassie come home*
Khat (Siamese cat) } Red Ned (horse) Major (cockatoo) Gyp (sheep dog) }	*Midnite* by Randolf Stow

Anatole (mouse)	Anatole series
Aslan (lion)	*The lion the witch and the wardrobe*
Babar (elephant)	*The story of Babar*
Basil (mouse)	*Basil of Baker Street*
Borka (goose)	*Borka; the adventures of a goose with no feathers*
Bunyip Bluegum (koala) } Sam Sawnoff (penguin) }	*The magic pudding* by Norman Lindsay
Jip (dog) } Gub Gub (pig) Dab Dab (duck) Chee Chee (monkey) Toto (dog) }	*The Dr. Dolittle stories* by Hugh Lofting
Pooh (bear) } Eeyore (donkey) Kanga (kangaroo) }	*The wizard of Oz Winnie the Pooh stories* by A. A. Milne
Ferdinand (bull)	*The story of Ferdinand*
Jemima Puddleduck (duck) } Mrs Tiggywinkle (hedgehog) Jeremy Fisher (frog) }	*Beatrix Potter characters*
Harry (dog)	*Harry the dirty dog*
Mog (cat)	*Meg and Mog* (series)

Paddington (bear)	*A bear called Paddington*	Teddy Robinson (bear)	*Teddy Robinson*
Rosie (hen)	*Rosie's walk*	Glory of the Republic (pig)	*The house of 60 fathers*
Stuart Little (mouse)	*Stuart Little*		

'Which colour?'

Snow (white) and Rose (red)
Baa Baa (black) sheep
Ten (green) bottles
Four and twenty (black) birds
The (silver) sword
The (red) balloon
Little boy (blue)
(Green) smoke
Encyclopedia (Brown)
(Blue) berries for Sal
The (golden) bird
(Grey) friars Bobby
(Ginger) Pye
(Black) Beauty
The Children of (Green) Knowe
The little (grey) men
The (grey) king
The (silver) chair
The land of (Green) Ginger
The (silver) crown
The (golden) fleece
When Hitler stole (pink) rabbit
Island of the (blue) dolphins
(Blue) Fin
(Green) eggs and ham
Little (Red) Riding Hood
Old (Yella)
A taste of (black) berries
(Black) hearts in Battersea
(Blue) beard
(Green) grow the rushes-O

20 questions about nursery rhymes for quizzes or puzzles.

1 Who did the dish run away with?
2 What did the queen eat in the parlour?
3 How did Mary's garden grow?
4 Who jumped over the moon?
5 What colour was Mary's lamb?
6 What did Simple Simon ask the pieman?
7 What did Jack and Jill go to fetch?
8 What did Jack Sprat like that his wife didn't?
9 Who sat down beside Miss Muffet?
10 What did 'the maiden all forlorn' do?
11 Where was Little Boy Blue when the cows and sheep got out?
12 Who had 'many a mile to go that night'?
13 What do you want to see when you ride to Banbury Cross?
14 What did Little Bo-Peep's sheep carry home with them?
15 When the boys come out to play, what does Georgie Porgie do?
16 Who had a great fall?
17 What did the old woman who lived in a shoe, give her children?
18 Why did Old Mother Hubbard go to the cupboard?
19 When the wind blows what happens to the cradle?
20 What did Tom the piper's son steal?

|| ||||
|
⑦

B.
|| ½ ½ ||
|
⑥

30 questions for literature games 'How many?'

1 The (3) little pigs
2 Snow White and the (7) dwarfs
3 How many bags full of wool? (3)
4 The wolf and the (7) little kids
5 The (7) ravens
6 The (12) days of Christmas
7 The (13) clocks (Thurber)
8 The (27th) annual African Hippo race (Lurie)
9 The (18th) emergency (Byars)
10 (7) little Australians (Turner)
11 (3) blind mice
12 The House of (60) Fathers (DeJong)
13 The (3) billy goats gruff
14 (4) and (20) blackbirds
15 The (21) balloons (Pene DuBois)
16 How many sheep did Bo-Peep lose? (all of them)
17 The (5) Chinese brothers (Bishop)
18 (500) hats of Bartholomew Cubbins (Suess)
19 (Millions) of cats (Gagg)
20 The (101) dalmations (Smith)
21 (1) (2) buckle my shoe
22 Dragonfall (5) (Ernshaw)
23 Jacob (2) (2) meets the hooded Fang (Richter)
24 Rub-dub-dub (3) men in a tub
25 (100) million francs (Berna)
26 Around the word in (80) days (Verne)
27 Goldilocks and the (3) bears
28 Ali Baba and the (40) thieves
29 The (29) steps (Buchan) *39*
30 The (3) Robbers (Ungerer)

20 questions for literature games 'Who Said?'

1 I'm late: I'm late! (White Rabbit from Alice)
2 My, what big eyes you have. (Wolf from Red Riding Hood)
3 I'll huff and I'll puff and I'll blow your house down (Wolf in Three Pigs)
4 I must leave the ball by midnight (Cinderella)
5 This bed is too hard. (Goldilocks)
6 Are all the children in their beds, it's past 8 o'clock. (Wee Willie Winkle)
7 Fee Fi Fo Fum. (Giant in Jack and the Beanstalk)
8 Wasn't it fun in the bath tonight? (Christopher Robin)
9 Mirror, mirror on the wall (Wicked Queen in Snow White)
10 Who's that walking over my bridge? (Troll from Three billy goats gruff).
11 What a good boy am I! (Little Jack Horner)
12 Yes sir! Yes sir! Three bags full. (Baa Baa black sheep)
13 Let me taste your wares. (Simple Simon)
14 The sky is falling. I must go and tell the king. (Chicken Little)
15 Let down your hair. (Prince in Rupunzel)
16 Today I'll brew and then I'll bake
Tomorrow I shall the queen's child take
How lucky I am that nobody knows
My name is _____
(Rumplestiltskin)
17 Bring me my pipe and my bowl and fiddlers three. (Old King Cole).
18 An elephant's faithful one hundred per cent. (Horton)
19 Some pig! (Charlotte's Web)
20 Romeo, Romeo, wherefore art thou Romeo? (Juliet)